D0390846

More Praise for *Laughter, Tears, Silence*

"No matter what you think about meditation, read this book. It offers a revolutionary look at a perennial topic and insight and suggestions that can stimulate anyone toward a deeper experience of inner peace, love, and joy."

— Marcia Wieder, CEO and founder of Dream University®

"Pragito Dove makes meditation fun for anyone. Her experience spans decades and she can help you discover your passion, live with courage, see your confidence explode and your creativity awaken."

— David Wood, senior vice president and
chief training officer of Isagenix International

"For over twenty years, I have been involved in the therapeutic humor arena. I have also worked with people who were dying and I practice Vipassana meditation. I have never thought of connecting these seemingly diverse elements. Yet, in a very masterful way, Pragito Dove has not only connected them but she also provides many easy-to-use meditative techniques that help you see the value in laughter, tears, and silence, and also help you find joy and peace in your life."

— Allen Klein, author of *The Healing Power of Humor*
and *The Courage to Laugh*

"The strength and simplicity of Pragito's insights and encouragement, her brilliant tapestry of techniques and extraordinary understanding allow her to work at great depth yet with lightness. Powerful, life-changing meditations are made accessible through Pragito's calm grace, compassion, generosity, and clarity. Working with the meditations in this practical, engaging book feels like walking an important path with a kind, loving, gentle, very wise guide at my side."

— Steve Wilson, founder of World Laughter Tour, Inc.

"Pragito Dove's meditations are an invitation to come home to that 'quiet place' that offers rest and restoration far from the rapid pace of modern life. Her book is truly transformational, jam-packed with insights and wisdom . . . useful and empowering."

— Ann J. Mincey, vice president of global communications (retired) of Redken 5th Avenue NYC and author of *Get Glowing*

"*Laughter, Tears, Silence* breaks the stereotype by introducing alternate techniques that promote active expression as well as silence. By unlocking your own laughter, tears, and inner peace you are catapulted into long-lasting joy and can experience the full spectrum of a vibrant life."

— Saranne Rothberg, CEO of the ComedyCures Foundation and stage IV cancer survivor

"Pragito Dove's approach takes into account the stress of modern life, and her meditations are tailor-made for those looking for ways to become more attuned to each moment of each day."

— Deva Premal and Miten, musicians and recording artists

LAUGHTER,
TEARS,
SILENCE

LAUGHTER, TEARS, SILENCE

Expressive Meditations to
Calm Your Mind
and Open Your Heart

PRAGITO DOVE

New World Library
Novato, California

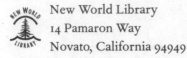

New World Library
14 Pamaron Way
Novato, California 94949

Copyright © 2010 by Pragito Dove

All rights reserved. This book may not be reproduced in whole or in part, stored in a retrieval system, or transmitted in any form or by any means — electronic, mechanical, or other — without written permission from the publisher, except by a reviewer, who may quote brief passages in a review.

Text design by Tona Pearce Myers

Library of Congress Cataloging-in-Publication Data
Dove, Pragito.
Laughter, tears, silence : expressive meditations to calm your mind and open your heart / Pragito Dove.
   p.   cm.
Includes bibliographical references and index.
ISBN 978-1-57731-683-1 (pbk. : alk. paper)
1. Meditation. 2. Osho, 1931–1990. I. Title.
BP605.R342D678 2010
204'.35—dc22   2009049579

First printing, February 2010
ISBN 978-1-57731-683-1
Printed in Canada on 100% postconsumer-waste recycled paper

g New World Library is a proud member of the Green Press Initiative.

10 9 8 7 6 5 4 3 2 1

To you, my reader:
May your life be filled with love, joy, and success

Contents

Part III: Silence   119

Part IV: Moving Forward   177

Meditations

Introduction

Part I: Laughter

Part II: Tears

Part III: Silence

Part IV: Moving Forward

Introduction

Do you sometimes feel that things are so chaotic around you
that you can't find your way to inner peace and calm? The
idea for this book came to me one day when I felt surrounded by
family craziness and was able to drop down into a still, silent place
within and just allow everything to be the way it was. I found balance in the midst of chaos.

From my years of experience with the meditation techniques
in this book, I have discovered that we can all be like a still pond
in the midst of a hurricane — the surface waters are slightly ruffled, but at the bottom all is calm, silent, and still. From this place
no sound can disturb us; no chaos, inner or outer, can pull us off
balance. When we are rooted in our inner silence we cannot be
tossed around like a ship without an anchor. We can surf the
waves, enjoying the ride, with our anchor of silence to ground us.

Through the techniques in this book you unburden yourself
from mental overload, emotional turmoil, and physical stress —
and you can have fun doing it! As these disturbances are gradually
released from your body and mind, you begin to experience the
serenity of the silence that lies hidden underneath.

Before I found the meditation techniques in this book, I often
felt out of control. My childhood was difficult and painful, and by

the time I was in my twenties I was a mess. My mother ruled our household through fear. Being her child was often a terrifying and intimidating experience. Saturday and Sunday lunches were the worst. The family sat at the dining table until everyone had finished eating. I longed for some noise, some distraction that would take the attention away from me and the brussels sprouts I hated. My father wouldn't have minded if I didn't eat them, I'm sure, but he was as afraid of my mother as my sister and I were. Unspoken anger pervaded the silence. The lunch table was supposed to be a place for us to be together, yet no one was comfortable or happy.

My problems weren't confined to mealtimes. My mother was difficult to please and had sudden bursts of inexplicable rage. She could be kind one moment, an invective-spewing tyrant the next. She had a habit of gliding silently around the house in soft-soled slippers and suddenly coming into my room to "surprise" me. I was terrified because I never knew when she might suddenly spring up and verbally attack me in some way. Living with her was like living in a war zone, and I felt in constant danger. I didn't know how to fight this war. It was a constant game of hide and dodge. It wasn't until she was ninety-four years old that my mother was diagnosed with a psychotic illness and agreed to take medication.

The turning point for me came when my son was born. Have you ever experienced a pivotal moment when you made a life-altering decision? I realized that unless I took myself in hand and committed to self-healing, I would transmit to him the anger, pain, and fear that had built up inside me like a dormant volcano waiting to explode. I did not want to put him through what I had experienced, so I started searching for techniques that would help me. I never considered meditation because I thought it meant sitting in silence with a rigid back for hours on end, and that was the last thing I felt like doing. Then I heard about the range of expressive meditation techniques created by twentieth-century mystic

Osho, including the Osho Mystic Rose meditation, Osho Dynamic, Dancing, and Shaking, and I decided they were worth a try. They worked! They were not only doable but also fun, and they awoke in me the long-buried joyful person who was longing to be happy, creative, loving, and loved. The rest, as they say, is history.

This book covers a range of techniques that follow no one tradition but draw on many. These include the unique expressive meditation techniques created by Osho, cutting-edge combinations of expression and stillness designed to help relieve the mental, physical, and emotional stresses of our noisy, hectic lifestyles and bring us in touch with our inner silence. Various Sufi techniques that explore the meeting of movement, sound, and silence are presented, as well as Buddhist, Tibetan Buddhist, Gurdjieffian, and other Eastern and Western practices. Throughout you will also find tales drawn from various people's experiences with laughter, tears, and silence. These stories are included to inspire and encourage you to find your own way to that silent place we all have within us, where we can rest with a sense of the absolute serenity and completeness of each moment.

How This Book Is Organized

Laughter, humor, and enjoyment of life come first, in part 1, because they are the easiest. No skill is needed, and there are no rules. Laughter is something you already know how to do — it's simply a matter of degree, of bringing more lightness into your life.

Although I'm sure you know that laughter is good for you, you might feel that you have nothing to laugh about, and you may even feel more like crying. Whether you are going through a difficult phase or just feel that life is hard, laughing might seem impossible. If this is the case, then part 2, which offers deeper practices to heal pain and grief, might resonate more with you right now. Getting out from under the weight of sorrow that you may have carried around for years brings deep relaxation, more love, and inner peace.

As you allow more laughter and tears into your life you are creating an even greater capacity for silence, peace, and spiritual nurturing. In part 3 we look at the many benefits of silence and silence practices. Attaining balance isn't always easy, but that doesn't mean we can't have it. It means we have to adjust our thinking and discover new, creative ways to find it. Silence is a powerful force for our well-being. It is that place inside us where wisdom, clarity, and calm reside. We can discover our passions and find meaning, purpose, and joy.

Finally, in part 4, I offer encouragement, inspiration, and practical plans to help you implement what you have discovered in this book. It's one thing to read the book but quite another to bring our dreams into reality. Otherwise they remain just that — dreams. As the new you emerges and unfolds you can step into the reality of your wishes, hopes, and dreams coming true, because they can!

In each part you will find different types of meditation techniques: expressive meditations (some of these require more time commitment), four-minute meditations, and some that are simply called meditations because they can be done in any amount of time.

Meditation and You

Meditation is not something apart from your everyday life; it is a quality, a way of being. Any activity done with awareness is meditation. It is not the activity that is important but your awareness as you do the activity. For example, when you take your morning shower, are you fully present? Or are you thinking about the day ahead? When *you* are fully present, enjoying the hot water on your body refreshing and invigorating you, then *meditation* is present. You can apply this focus of being fully present to any activity.

Then you will be able to easily and naturally incorporate meditation into your day.

The purpose here is not to cut yourself off from life but rather to enter more deeply and fully into it. Through laughter, tears, and silence you can bring a more authentic quality to your relationships. You can experience both being alone with yourself and being with others in a more deeply fulfilling way. Contrary to what many people believe, meditation and relationships are not mutually exclusive. In fact, they enhance each other. When you spend time alone getting to know yourself, you are then available for more authentic togetherness with others.

Inner peace is possible for us all. My intention here is to show you how to discover the joy, wisdom, and silence that reside within you. Meditation is not a technique. Rather, the techniques are there to serve as a bridge to bring you home to your authentic self. Meditation is where we arrive (our destination), and the techniques are how we get there (our vehicle(s) of choice for the journey).

These techniques link the sacred in us with our day-to-day existence. We are spiritual beings in a physical body. We don't want to be in denial either of our spirituality or of our physicality because then we are not whole; we are divided. It is this division that creates stress, dis-ease, and unhappiness, an inner fight. My intention is to show you how to come to wholeness, to bring you to a peaceful coexistence within yourself.

There are three essentials to any meditation technique: relaxation (more on p. 127), nonjudgment (more on p. 138), and witnessing (more on p. 142). I have included a short technique here as an example of what is to come and to help you get started. Over time, as you get used to this technique, and as your understanding of what meditation is and what it is not deepens, you will naturally and easily be able to incorporate the three essentials into your practices and into your life.

⬡ FOUR-MINUTE MEDITATION: *The Three Essentials*

BENEFITS

As you make a regular practice of the three essentials (you can start with one minute a day), you will find yourself discovering a deep calm, relaxation, and inner peace that permeate your entire day.

The Three Essentials contains three vital components. First, allow the body to be relaxed. Second, witness with a relaxed awareness whatever is going on, without any interference, without any fight with the mind, any attempt to control the mind, any concentration. Third, watch the mind and your emotions, silently, without any judgments or evaluation.

When you incorporate these three things, slowly, slowly, a great silence descends over you. Start now for one minute, sit with eyes closed, body relaxed and watch with no judgment.

Meditation is awareness. It's that simple. It's about living in the here and now instead of allowing the mind to take you into the future or the past. The techniques in this book help you come into the present and integrate body and spirit. Whether it's through laughter, tears, or silence, or all three, you find your own way home. It was the laughter and expressive techniques that showed me that meditation can be fun. My definition of a spiritual person is someone who is spirited, has a zest for life out of the sheer joy of being alive in her body. This kind of positive vibration enhances the quality of your life and the lives of those around you. Further, I have discovered a powerful connection between meditation and focus that I would like to share with you now.

Enhance Your Ability to Focus

Would you like to be more focused, confident, and relaxed, even in the midst of chaos? Or have you ever found yourself distracted in a situation in which you needed to be focused? An ability to focus and be highly productive is one of the greatest benefits I can attribute to a consistent practice of these meditation techniques.

Let's define the word *focus*. Think about this: when you take a magnifying glass, aligning it with the sun's rays and focusing it on a piece of paper, at some point the paper will catch fire. You have harnessed the power of the sun's rays for a specific result. This illustrates the power of harnessing your energy to focus on something specific to get a very powerful outcome. Not that I am suggesting that you set fire to everything in sight! But once you understand how to do this with your own energy, everything becomes possible for you. Focus is a quality you can bring to any activity, a quality of relaxed alertness, presence, clarity of mind, and creativity. It means being 100 percent present. Imagine, for example, walking along a beach, feeling the warmth of the sun on your skin, listening to the waves crashing on the shore, aware of the sand touching your feet, tasting the salty tang of the sea air, seeing the blues of the sky and sea and the yellow of the sand. All fives senses are involved with enjoying every moment. You are fully present in this in-the-body experience.

Why are we so easily distracted? Have you ever been in a meeting or talking with your partner and found yourself drifting when you knew you were supposed to be focusing? Why does that happen to us? Because we are full to overflowing with mental clutter, emotional turmoil, and physical stress, and it just plain *is* difficult to stay focused.

Would you like to know how to eliminate all that inner clutter?

Do the expressive meditation techniques offered in this book. The Gibberish meditation (p. 65), for example, allows you to dump out mental overload and physical and emotional stress so that your mind is fresh and uncluttered. The Laughter (p. 9) and Osho Dynamic meditations (p. 70) are great for releasing emotional, physical, and mental turmoil, resulting in calm, peace, and a greater ability to focus.

As you clear out all this clutter you attain clarity of mind, you gain emotional integrity, and you gain greater access to your sense of humor and creativity. Your ability to focus greatly increases for longer periods of time.

Meditation is a quality of presence, clarity of mind, creativity. It means being 100 percent present. You can bring to any activity that quality of relaxed alertness.

Do you remember? This is exactly how we defined *focus*!

Sitting Postures

For the techniques in this book that involve sitting, I would like to offer some suggestions. First, and most important, do not force a posture. If you're not comfortable, this simply creates more tension and nothing is achieved. If you can sit, good, but if it is a strain, take some other position. If you cannot sit on the ground, then sit on a chair.

Take some care, of course, but don't worry too much about whether or not your spine is absolutely erect. It is too easy to become preoccupied with these minor things.

Understand what a posture should look like, and try to absorb that, then continue on your way. The essential thing is that you are comfortable and at ease.

In the sitting positions, you want your hips to be higher than your knees to keep the stress off your back. Try placing a cushion under your hips to raise them up. You don't have to sit ramrod straight; doing so will make you tense. Sitting comfortably for a meditation technique gives you a chance to get in touch with how much you like yourself. You want to feel that your back and head are upright and in alignment, showing a sense of dignity.

How to Use This Book

In every chapter you'll discover simple, easy techniques that you can do right now as you're reading. In addition, each chapter is full of motivating and empowering words to help keep you focused. And each chapter gives you empowering insights that leave you with actionable steps and thoughts to keep you focused on your dreams and on creating your life, just as you want it to be.

You'll gain the belief, confidence, and motivation necessary to go after your deepest, most passionate desires, whether they be for wealth, family enrichment, a lasting legacy, or anything else your heart desires.

I suggest that you read the book slowly, giving yourself time to absorb and try out different meditations. The meditations can be done alone or with a friend or in a group. It is purely a matter of personal preference. Some of you may prefer to use this book in conjunction with a meditation class or to start your own class. We each have to discover for ourselves which meditation techniques we enjoy and where and when to practice them. Some of the techniques, but not all of them, require you to sit in silence.

May this book encourage you to find the compassion and creativity that shine within you. May it bring you love, joy, and great success.

PART ONE

Laughter

I start this book with the topic of laughter and with laughter meditations, because this is how I discovered that meditation can be fun. In my experience the laughter practice is one of the easiest ways to get into meditation. Even if this is the only technique you do, it will transform your life and your world; in fact, this technique can transform the whole world. You can start with a smile or a chuckle, and even if you just do one minute each day, you experience profound benefits. You attract good things, improve your health, lower your stress level, open your heart to more love, and unleash your creative juices. We've all felt it, haven't we — that overwhelming sensation of laughter when each fiber of our being pulsates with joy, bringing on a deep feeling of relaxation? Out of this easiness everything is possible, because instead of a lack of energy, you experience the fullness of energy without tension. The more relaxed you become, the fresher you feel, full of potential for creativity. Laughter is an immensely valuable activity; it is life, love, and light. When real belly laughter happens it comes from your very core. Have you experienced this? From your very center ripples start spreading outward. It is almost like an earthquake! Laughter brings energy from your inner source to your surface. It is a mystery, and it's better to experience it than to hear someone talk about it, isn't it?

Most of us hope for these moments of happy abandon, and we may tell ourselves that they don't happen often enough. The truth is, we don't have to wait to be happy. The concepts and practices I've included here are designed to help us relax, loosen up, and enjoy life. They provide an opportunity for playfulness and a reminder that life does not have to be a constant struggle. Even when we are not feeling happy, these techniques can help energize us and move us forward in difficult times. They help coax to the surface our inner happiness, serving as a vehicle to awaken us to our innate joy.

Happiness is our essential nature. Rather than waiting for events outside us to determine our happiness, we can find deep inside the happiness that is our essential nature. Perhaps we think that we have to be relaxed and calm and that all sorts of conditions need to be there for us to be happy. This is not the case. Happiness can be there *for no reason.* The more we make a practice of smiling, laughing, and enjoying ourselves for no reason, the more we discover we already have what we are seeking.

Meditation isn't something you have to work at with a straight face. Be sincere about meditation, yes, but not serious, because then you will be forcing yourself to achieve. This only creates more tension. The more fun you have with the various techniques — the more playful you are as you approach them — the more relaxed you are and the more you will want to keep meditating.

In his book *Laugh after Laugh: The Healing Power of Humor*, Dr. Raymond Moody explains: "Laughter is a good natural tranquilizer. It can stimulate the brain to produce hormones called catecholamines which may then trigger the release of endorphins. Endorphins have been described as a natural valium and foster a sense of relaxation and well being. Catecholamines also enhance blood flow and thus may speed healing, reduce inflammation and stimulate alertness."

Laughter's Benefits

Laughter is good for us in every way: physically, emotionally, spiritually. It offers many benefits:

- *Laughter stimulates physical healing.* If you can laugh when you are sick, you heal faster. If you cannot laugh, sooner or later you will become ill. Laughter brings energy from your inner source to your surface.

- *Laughter enhances our creativity.* I have noticed, after numerous episodes of laughter, that I become flooded with creative energy. As old conditioning is released, the unconscious opens and insights come. The relaxation of body and mind provides a gateway for inner wisdom to be expressed.

- *Laughter is rejuvenating and regenerating.* When we laugh and smile we loosen up and generally feel better. The face collects stress, and when we laugh we release a tremendous amount of tension, giving us a more youthful appearance. Laughing reminds us to have fun. Today, do something just for the sheer fun of it.

- *Laughter is sexy.* Laughter helps attract people who are good for us and is very beneficial for anyone who is sexually blocked. It releases inhibitions and opens us up, bringing us directly in touch with our life force energy. Many people have reported improved sexual responsiveness after doing the laughter meditations.

- *Laughter is good for relationships.* Humor draws people together. Many couples who do the Laughter (p. 9) and the Osho Mystic Rose (p. 50) meditations tell me that they find a tremendous improvement in their relating. They discover another side of each other, the playful, humorous side, which brings relief to the more serious parts of life concerned with work, money, housework, the kids, and so on. Remember the old adage "All work and no play makes Jack a dull boy"? Well, it doesn't do much for Jill either!

- *Laughter opens the heart.* Laughter creates an opening to the love, compassion, courage, trust, and intuitive wisdom that vibrate within you.
- *Laughter activates the Law of Attraction.* Laughter fills us with warm, positive vibrations that activate the feeling state we need to attract good things to us.
- *Laughter gives us a glimpse of freedom from the mind.* For those moments when you are totally laughing, you are free of the mind. You are brought from worry to humor, from tension to relaxation, from fear to trust, from timidity to courage. In other words, you move from the mind to the heart. You cannot think and laugh at the same time. In those seconds when you are out of the mind, you are in meditation. In those seconds the mind is not and you are.

You can even laugh your way to enlightenment. Laughter serves as a bridge to our inner silence. It is an ordinary experience that can give you an extraordinary experience, a glimpse of no-mind. It can be used as a preparation for meditation.

There is hope. There are solutions to depression, fear, and pain. We can experience our emotions in a safe, meditative context, so that we can be refreshed and renewed.

In this part I've included many techniques that helped me transform my anger, pain, and fear into love, creativity, and joy. The same can happen for you. You can do these meditations alone or with friends. Just do them. One minute a day is a good start.

Be kind and gentle with yourself. If you don't feel like laughing, practice smiling more often, read some joke books, or watch some comedies. As you do, what is naturally inside will begin to surface more and more easily. And remember, if you are going through a difficult time, you can also give an equal amount of time to allowing your sadness to be there. *It is the balanced awareness and expression of both these energies that will bring you to a deeper harmony and peace within yourself.*

THE HEALING POWER OF LAUGHTER

In my twenty-plus years of teaching a wide range of meditation techniques, the laughter meditation stands out as the most popular. I have never given a presentation in which nobody laughed or wanted to laugh. Even if they had never heard of this technique before, they were willing to jump in, after a short explanation, and just start laughing. Usually, just talking about laughter and the laughter meditation seems to open people up, and many start smiling and laughing before we have even started. Have you experienced that? For example, when someone asks if you've heard a certain joke, do you immediately feel laughter start to percolate in anticipation of the joke and exploding at the punch line? One of my students, Gisele, healed her fear of public speaking when she had to give a talk about the Laughter meditation. She kept laughing out of anxiety and ended up sharing the meditation in an unexpected way. Her audience couldn't stop laughing either, and all Gisele's problems, fears, and tensions dissolved as everyone united in spontaneous laughter. In her innocence, Gisele took everyone beyond the mind and straight into the heart of laughter itself. She won everyone over, because it is just so human, isn't it, to laugh when we are nervous? We have all experienced wanting to laugh inappropriately in church or on solemn occasions, and stuffing it down seems to make things even funnier. The Laughter meditation provides an appropriate way to release our tensions and just to laugh for the sake of laughing. Here is a short meditation technique to illustrate the many dimensions of us that laughter can reach.

MEDITATION: *Let Go of Ego*

BENEFITS

This technique helps you to drop deeper into your heart, deeper into trusting your inner wisdom. Sometimes failure happens to teach us to let go of ego and to move into a more authentic place in ourselves.

Notice if you feel bad because your ego has been crushed. This is a good thing. Have a good laugh. Do this whenever you feel your ego burning. Or maybe you would rather cry. Either way, expressing yourself this way will help take you beyond your ego.

Once I was invited to give a lunchtime presentation to employees of a large corporation in Northern California. In anticipation of the event, the director had hooked us up via video satellite to two branches of the company in Southern California. Everyone, men and women alike, was wearing a business suit, and it looked like it was going to be a serious meeting. But as we started the Laughter meditation (see description on p. 9), we were amazed at the volume of laughter that poured forth. One woman actually fell off her chair, she was laughing so much, and that made her, and everyone else, laugh even more. Afterward, the participants said they liked the idea of laughing with their colleagues, whom they could see on the screens. They all felt united, and they enjoyed this way of being in touch with one another.

I have noticed that as we do the Laughter meditation with others, any mask we are wearing gets stripped away. We are simply all human beings, laughing together. Boundaries dissolve between teacher and student, parent and child, boss and employee, and any other categories that the mind creates to judge people as "superior" or "inferior."

The Laughter meditation is powerful in its simple ability to transform and heal our relationships with ourselves and with others. It is good for us in every way: physically, emotionally, mentally, spiritually. Do it now. Start with smiling more, for no particular reason, just because! Laugh at every opportunity that presents itself; look for opportunities to laugh.

Below you will find a more detailed description of the Laughter meditation technique. However, remember that you can laugh anywhere, anytime, for any or for no reason at all. If you are in a situation where you cannot follow the instructions below exactly, it doesn't matter. The most important thing is that you bring more laughter, smiles, humor, joy, and lightness into your life. The technique described below is particularly good to do in a group, and by a group I mean at least two people. If you want to do this technique on your own, here are a few tips for you:

Start laughing, if you can, first thing in the morning when you get up, and last thing at night when you go to bed. This practice transforms the quality of your day. It also transforms the quality of your sleep. Your sleep is deeper, and you awaken more refreshed and relaxed. Laugh for no reason, at the ridiculousness of your life, of your day, rushing from here to there. It creates a domino effect — laughter leads to more laughter. Start and finish your day with laughter, and watch as you become more easygoing, more sincere, more creative, more youthful, more compassionate, more intuitive, more authentic, and more expansive.

Remember that at the beginning laughing in this way takes some effort, but after a little while it starts to happen naturally. Your body gets used to it and even starts to expect it.

Do it in the shower, while driving your car, while stuck in

traffic. "Ha! Ha! Ha!" Even to say those words out loud starts to transform your mood.

EXPRESSIVE MEDITATION: *Laughter* ◎

STAGE ONE: LAUGHTER

Raise both arms in the air, and shout "yahoo" several times. Then burst into laughter for absolutely no reason. Just start laughing. At the beginning it may seem weird, and you may have to force it a little, saying, "Ha, ha, ha" or "Ho, ho, ho" to get the energy of the laughter moving. You might want to use the laughter track of my *Laughter and Tears* CD to help you get started.*

Soon spontaneous laughter arises. Try it for thirty seconds, for one or two minutes, or for three or five minutes. Just laugh for no reason at all. Laugh for the sake of laughing.

It can be helpful to have some pillows to throw around and play with, depending on your situation. The idea is to become a child again and to experience the natural spontaneity and joy of life that we were all born with. That spontaneity and joy are still there; they've just been buried under all the to-do lists and the seriousness that we all learn comes with adulthood. But they don't have to be. We can reclaim our natural joy and playfulness, and then we become more productive, creative, and fun-loving adults.

A great way to generate more laughter is to speak in gibberish. Do not, however, use English or any other language that you understand. If you don't understand Italian, you can speak in Italian. By that I mean speak in gibberish with an Italian accent, and use your hands a lot to gesture. You can speak in Chinese or any kind of language, just as long as you don't understand it. You can make all kinds of sounds, and even repeat "yahoo" from time

---

* To order this CD or any of the others mentioned in this book, please see pages 206–7.

to time to reenergize yourself. It is your responsibility to keep yourself laughing. You don't have to be a stand-up comedian or help other people laugh, unless it is in a playful way that is also fun for you. The focus is on you and on keeping yourself laughing, whether you are alone or interacting with others.

For a more detailed description of doing the Laughter meditation in a group, see the Osho Mystic Rose meditation (p. 50).

STAGE TWO: SIT OR LIE DOWN IN SILENCE

The first thing to remember is not to get serious. Just because you are going to sit in silence with your eyes closed doesn't mean that you have to be serious. Sincere, yes, but not serious! Sit down, or lie down, if you prefer, and close your eyes. You might find, and many people do, that gales of laughter are still bubbling up from inside you.

That's okay. You can sit with eyes closed and a big smile on your face and allow the energy of the laughter to keep on coming, if it wants to. Don't force it to arise, and don't repress it. Simply allow the energy to naturally express itself, as laughter, as smiles, or as silence. The idea here is to experience the laughter *from the inside*. This is something we are not used to doing, since laughter is an extroverted activity, focused on what is outside ourselves. In this second stage we take the focus *within* to experience the energy of the laughter, and/or the effects of the laughter from stage one. After a while the laughter naturally comes to an end, and you feel yourself dropping down into a place of warm silence, stillness, and joy. Experience this feeling as totally as you can, because this is how, over time, you can use the energy of the laughter to take you deeper inside yourself to your center of wisdom, clarity, and love. This technique is one of the simplest and easiest ways to come home to yourself and to find that place of divine abiding where no person or situation can disturb you.

You can do this technique for any amount of time that you wish. For example: two minutes of laughter followed by two minutes of silence. Do the same amount of time for each stage. This helps keep the balance between the extroverted nature of stage one and the introverted nature of stage two. *It is the balanced awareness and expression of both these energies that will bring you to a deeper harmony and peace within yourself.*

HOTEI: THE LAUGHING BUDDHA

The enlightened mystic most associated with laughter is Hotei, also known as the laughing buddha. Hotei was a large man with a big belly who travelled from village to village in sixteenth-century Japan. He had no desire to call himself a Zen master or to gather disciples. Instead he walked the streets carrying a sack full of candy, fruit, and doughnuts, which he gave to all the children who gathered around him. And he laughed — a lot!

At first people would gather around him because they thought he was mad to laugh so much. But Hotei's laugher was so contagious that soon they all found themselves doubled over with laughter, and they forgot all their judgments. Even when they asked him questions about enlightenment, Hotei would just laugh. Soon they forgot their questions, the laughter was so infectious. The people started to wait for Hotei. After laughing with such totality, they found that all their senses had sharpened. Their whole being had become lighter, as if a great burden had been lifted. With Hotei they laughed for no reason at all. And yet everyone was nourished and cleansed by the laughter and felt a deep sense of well-being. Something from the unknowable depth started ringing bells in people's hearts.

It is said that Hotei even laughed in his sleep, that his whole body would shake as the laughter rumbled up from his belly. Hotei was very stout and strong because he laughed so much. Laughter was so natural to him that anything and everything helped him to laugh. This was his way of teaching enlightenment. And as they shared the laughter with him, people felt that they were in the presence of a master, that something of tremendous significance was transpiring. So he came to be known as the laughing buddha. He was a different type of master from the Buddha, but he was a buddha nonetheless. He offered another way, through laughter. He was his own message. His life was his teaching.

Hotei didn't laugh at jokes or at others. He laughed at himself. He laughed in celebration of existence, out of joy of life. And he was tremendously compassionate. He wanted to share his gift with as many people as possible. He wanted to see people's faces light up with laughter, see their beings become radiantly happy at the sheer joy of being alive.

Hotei had no philosophy, scriptures, dogmas, theories, ideologies, or concepts to preach. His teaching was existential. He wanted everyone to experience the joy that laughter brings. This kind of meditation is not something that can be talked about. It must be experienced. Hotei was doing a tremendous service to humanity. He was not a philosopher. He was a very simple being, silent, happy, alive, living moment to moment.

One day Hotei was passing through a village. He sat down under a tree, with his eyes closed, not laughing, not even smiling, completely calm and peaceful. A villager asked him: "You are not laughing, Hotei?"

He opened his eyes and said, "I am preparing." The villager did not understand. He said, "What do you mean by preparing?"

Hotei replied: "I have to prepare myself for laughter. I have to rest. I have to go within. I have to forget the whole world so that I can recharge, and then I can be filled with laughter again."

If you really want to laugh totally you must also spend time sitting in silence. If you really want to laugh, you must learn about the relationship between laughter and tears. The more you laugh, the more you can cry, and vice versa. Have you ever experienced that sometimes you laugh so hard the tears come and that sometimes, when you are crying, laughter suddenly appears? These two energies are deeply connected, and out of these polarities you find your balance. Your inner silence goes even deeper. Then life is a dance. You can laugh, you can cry, you can be silent, you can be ecstatic, you can be still.

Find Your Inner Hotei

How do we intentionally bring ourselves to laughter? Jokes are a great place to start. They are never logical. They bring us into the present moment. We forget our seriousness, our problems, and for a moment we are innocent children again, full of wonder and awe.

The reason we laugh at jokes is that they take sudden twists and turns. When you start to hear a joke your mind is functioning logically. You expect logical things to happen, and then something comes along that you could not have imagined. It is illogical, ridiculous, absurd. The shock . . . and then you explode into laughter. A certain kind of tension has been released.

The purpose of the joke is not the joke itself — it is the laughter that follows. When you laugh you are no longer in your head. And after the laughter, you can drop into a profound silence. Do this with a friend(s).

⊙ FOUR-MINUTE MEDITATION: *Sit under a Tree*

BENEFITS

Something as simple as this four-minute technique can be wonderfully effective at helping you to feel more rooted in yourself, more grounded, and at the same time more open, receptive, and relaxed. As you regenerate your energy, you will find your natural, spontaneous laughter welling back up to the surface.

If you want to get grounded, there's no better way to do it than by sitting under a tree with your eyes closed. Try it. Feel the breeze as it passes through the tree, rustling the leaves and branches. The wind touches you, moves around you, and passes by you. Now allow it to move within you and pass through you. With your eyes closed, feel that you are also like a tree, open, with the wind blowing through you — not passing by your side but right through you.

If you can't find a tree, sit on the ground in your backyard, in the park, or on the beach. A place outdoors is best. If, however, you are reading this in freezing sub-zero temperatures or in sweltering heat, just sit on the floor indoors. Imagine the tree. It works just as well.

PLAY

Along with all the laughter, a playfulness I had not known I possessed began to resurface. I started to relax, loosen up, and enjoy life more. I was reminded that life does not have to be a constant struggle. *I became a child again.* By that I mean not that I became childish, but that my childlike qualities of wonder, awe, innocence, excitement, and imagination, which had been buried, started to resurface. I discovered within an extraordinary capacity to be playful — that it was a quality woven like a thread into the tapestry of my life.

To become more real in our lives, we have to go back to the point when we stopped being authentically ourselves. For many of us, this happened the first time we became angry or upset and our parents told us, "Don't be angry! Don't be upset!" We were expressing perfectly natural feelings, but we learned right then and there that we paid a price for being true to ourselves.

I began to regain that wondrous quality of childhood by discovering the point when I started being "good" rather than natural. I began to remove the masks of personality, because they had become a prison, a false identity I had put on like a coat, to conform to what the rest of the world wanted me to be.

Being playful, you might be thinking, doesn't that mean being irresponsible? On the contrary, I think we avoid responsibility when it's connected with something like a duty or a burden, something we don't really feel connected to or care about. When we are having fun, being playful, our life energy is activated; with its being allowed to flow freely, we will *naturally feel responsible* for what we are initiating through our creative participation. Fun doesn't have to be something we do outside our work time; rather, fun *fuels* our work and unleashes our creativity.

Look at children: they are always bubbling over with energy because *to a child everything is play*. Children don't think of the past — they have no past to think about. They are not worried about the future, because they have no time consciousness. They live totally unworried, in the moment. Through using the techniques in this book, I relearned to remain true to the moment. The inner silence gained through doing these practices can give you a new childhood, a new innocence, a new festivity. We too can take everything as play. Ultimately your life will become one big playground.

Our educational system prepares us for competition, making failure difficult to accept. We become too concerned that the whole world is watching us. No one has enough time for others, because they are too wrapped up in winning.

We can learn as much from failure as we can from victory. And when another person wins, we can rejoice in her victory too. Our failure is a defeat only if we did not put our whole energy into it. We can learn humbleness and to accept whatever life brings us. And we can learn compassion, for ourselves and others. All these things bring us maturity.

We all need to master basic skills: basketball players have to be able to pass the ball, shoot baskets, and have good footwork, timing, and rhythm. Tennis players must practice their serve, lobs, and volleys. Even the great Spanish cellist Pablo Casals said that he spent the first three hours every day practicing his scales. Phil Jackson, coach of the champion LA Lakers, stated that we master basic skills *so* that players can be intuitive and play without thinking. The mind and the ego disappear, and only playing remains.

How can we apply Jackson's method to our lives? For starters, we can understand the difference between a game and play. When play becomes serious, it becomes a game. Play is not concerned with goals. When you forget about goals, then herenow playfulness starts growing in you. *Playfulness is not then and there: it is herenow.* You have just to be. When a serious person starts playing, the play can turn into a game. And when a playful person plays a game, she can enjoy it as play. She can delight in each moment, and whether she wins or loses the game, she will be content because she has enjoyed herself. *With play everyone is a winner.*

If you are playing to win, you play with tension and anxiety. You are not concerned with play itself and its joy; you are more concerned with the outcome. Live your life as play. Death takes everything away, whether you win or lose. The only thing that matters is how you play the game. Did you enjoy it — the game itself? Then each moment is joyful. *Don't sacrifice the present moment for the future.* Live with immense joy, and die with immense joy. This is how a person who meditates has to be: once you know the art and ecstasy of living, you then know the art and ecstasy of dying.

And this very enjoyment and playfulness can lead us into the silence, which is at the core of meditation. Silence can arise in utter playfulness, when you are not seeking anything, when you are simply dancing or singing or chanting; when you are not asking, when no future is evoked. Silence, meditation, "the zone" is happening. You cannot snatch it from the universe's hands; you cannot desire it and then attain it. You can do only one thing: you can become an empty receiver — and that's what happens when you are playful. Down through the ages we have been taught this: Don't laugh, don't dance, don't be playful! Life is a serious affair! When you take a playful approach to life, you can learn a new language, equating meditation with fun, prayer with love, playfulness and laughter with the divine. We can share what existence has given us and dance and hold hands and be drunk with life and utterly absorbed in the moment. That is the meaning of fun, of laughter, of joy: to be utterly absorbed in the moment — as if no other moment exists. And it doesn't.

Happiness can exist for no reason at all. The more we make a practice of smiling, laughing, being playful, enjoying ourselves *for no reason*, the more we discover that what we seek we already have.

If you want to find joy, let go of winning and losing. When you drop down to a deeper level, you discover a place where no one wins and no one loses — you experience being together in love and friendship.

FOUR-MINUTE MEDITATION: *Enjoy Yourself!*

BENEFITS

The key to this technique is this: find something that you enjoy. Because whenever you enjoy something you are in tune with yourself and in harmony with the universe. You are connected to your center, your inner haven of serenity. You discover that what you are seeking is already within you, that it has nothing to do with the future, that it is already here now.

This technique is very simple. *Only do what you enjoy.* Do this whenever you have an opportunity, maybe on your lunch break or during the weekend. Enjoyment comes from the center, so whenever we are doing something we enjoy, we are centered, we feel a deep inner peace arising, we are relaxed.

Check in with yourself to determine whether you are doing something because it is a duty or because you were taught to like it or because you are truly enjoying yourself. And the possibilities are vast and individual, so you are bound to find something that you enjoy.

Experiment. If you are walking along the road, bring your awareness to your activity. Are you enjoying your walk? If not, then stop. Do something else.

Become like a small child — dancing, singing, laughing — and silence comes to you unawares. That's what God is. God is not in the scriptures but in our loved ones' eyes, in the flowers and the rivers and the stars. God is everywhere, and we find God through playfulness. Playfulness brings us alive. Seriousness cripples us, and we live in a straitjacket, behind iron walls. We have to drop out of the mind, which is full of old conditioning. And by doing so, suddenly we find we have always been in the land of play: not for a single moment had we left it — nobody can leave it. We just forget about it. We become serious, and we forget.

We are still the children playing on the beach by the ocean. We are still searching for seashells on the beach, collecting wild flowers, trying to catch hold of a butterfly. That purity of childhood has not been taken away from us — it has only been blocked by seriousness, by ego, by mind. The rock is blocking the fountain, but the fountain has not disappeared. Remove the rock, and the fountain flows again in all its splendor.

✦ FOUR-MINUTE MEDITATION: *Feel Joy Rising in Your Heart*

BENEFITS

Whenever you can remain centered in your inner joy, you have a different attitude about everything. You become joy itself, and you experience a great change within. The joy spreads through your whole being, and your awareness deepens it.

Suddenly you see a friend you have not seen for many days, and you feel joy arising in your heart. But you are focused on your friend, not on your joy. You are missing something, and your joy is fleeting.

Next time you see a friend and suddenly feel joyful, concentrate on this joy. Feel it and become it, and meet the friend while being aware of and filled with your joy. Be present for your friend, and at the same time, remain centered in your happiness.

You can try this technique in many situations: while watching the sun rise, greeting your pet, playing ball with your child, watching a leaf float to the ground. Be centered in your joy. Instead of being object centered, become self-centered. Many people think that when we feel joy, the cause is external. That is not the case. *Joy is always within you.* The external situation has simply triggered the joy within you.

FOUR-MINUTE MEDITATION: *Playfulness Is Here Now* ☼

BENEFITS

This technique enhances your lightness of spirit, creativity, and joy.

Whatever playfulness means to you, engage in it. Whether it's playing indoor or outdoor games, watching comedies, or taking your dog to the park, if it turns you on, go for it. Being around children reawakens the magical qualities of presence, joy, and laughter.

Look at your life and see where you can bring in more fun: at work, at home, with friends, with your partner. Whenever you are doing an "unfun" activity, such as waiting in line at the grocery store, sitting in traffic, or tackling a difficult report at your desk, see if you can change your attitude. Find a way to bring a playful quality to your situation: strike up a positive conversation with the next person in line, make exasperated (but smiling!) gestures to your fellow drivers, bring some humor to your report, or stand up from time to time, stretch and smile, then sit down again and continue the report. Do whatever works for you and your situation. Be creative. Then the chances are very good that you'll write a great report, arrive home in a good mood, and make new friends.

⚙ FOUR-MINUTE MEDITATION: *Living a Life of Joy*

BENEFITS

> *The truly conscious person lives each moment for the sheer joy of living — there is no motive, no desire, no ambition. Sometimes it is cloudy, and sometimes it is sunny. Sometimes it is quiet, and sometimes it is noisy. Things are as they are, and we can start enjoying whatever is in the moment.*

STEP ONE

Live in the moment for the sheer joy of living it. When you do, each moment has a quality of ecstasy. Whatever the moment contains — joy, disappointment, sadness, excitement — welcome it. Don't try to force it or change it; just allow it to be. If you have just lost your job, or failed an exam, or discovered your best friend is relocating to a faraway city, the first step is acceptance.

STEP TWO

Now see the situation as an opportunity to create something new, to stay aware that an even better situation awaits you. The more you can accept whatever the moment brings, whether or not you like it, the more opportunities you have to tap into joy.

THE ART OF CELEBRATION

I was raised to believe that life was a painful struggle. Despite this, when as a child I used to look out of my bedroom window at the poplar trees in our neighbor's backyard, something would stir in my heart. I could see the sun glittering on the leaves of the trees as they swayed in the wind as if they were dancing, having fun, enjoying being poplar trees. Something told me that life could be that way for me too. I didn't know how at that young age, but I trusted that when I grew up I would find out.

What were you raised to believe about life? Did you learn that people drag themselves through life as if it is a burden, a duty to be performed? Do you feel that you have to "get through" life? Your authentic self has been covered in so many layers of culture, etiquette, education, religion, and country that you have completely forgotten that you are here to grow, that you are here to become a beautiful green tree full of fruit, flowers, and fragrance, dancing in the wind, rain, and sun.

Make your life a dance. Let it be a celebration. Take your guidance from nature. Open your heart. The dance of the trees cannot be understood by the head; the heart has to be open for it.

Perhaps this idea makes us feel guilty. How can life really be that good when we have been taught, as I was, that it is a vale of sorrows? Here is how I learned to drop guilt and live a life of celebration.

Drop Guilt, and Celebrate Instead

First let's define guilt. Guilt is self-judgment. Let's say, for example, that you decide to go to the movies. Instead of enjoying it, you sit through the film criticizing yourself for being in a movie instead of working, working out, or getting exercise in the fresh air. Result: you don't fully enjoy the movie, nor do you do any of the things you were berating yourself about.

Practice the following technique to help you shift gears, drop guilt, and celebrate what you are doing each moment.

⚙ FOUR-MINUTE MEDITATION: *Dropping Guilt*

BENEFITS

This technique helps you celebrate and enjoy each moment, whatever you are doing, wherever you are.

STEP ONE

Notice, with nonjudgment and compassion for yourself, the self-critical thoughts passing through your mind. These are usually accompanied by the words *should* and *ought*: "I should have gone to exercise at the gym," "I ought to be cleaning out the kitchen cupboards"— instead of sitting right here enjoying this movie!

STEP TWO

Remind yourself that downtime and fun are vital to your well-being.

The more you keep yourself in a positive, celebratory state of mind, the more you relax and attract good things to you. The more you stay in the present moment while watching a movie, for example, the more you enjoy it, which is energizing and revitalizing.

In addition, after the movie, for example, you experience more joy and more energy for exercising, cleaning, and sharing with friends and family!

The greedy, fear-based mind can keep us on a treadmill of constant striving to achieve goals. Once one goal is accomplished, it's on to the next one. The following practice helps you step out of this cycle and revolutionize your state of mind.

FOUR-MINUTE MEDITATION: *Celebrate Yourself*   ⟐

BENEFITS

Celebrations are a constant reminder to your mind to think positive thoughts. They change your attitude to life. Eventually, every moment of your life becomes a celebration, a dance, a joy.

Choose one thing to celebrate about yourself: your health, your positive attitude in doing this practice, your willingness to try new things. It doesn't matter what you are celebrating, only that you are celebrating yourself. You can celebrate the same thing every day, or find different things.

However big or small the occasion, look for excuses to be in a state of celebration. You can celebrate failures too.

Add One Thing to Your Life: Celebration

We are taught to keep adding things to our lives, to buy the latest technology, a newer car, more clothes, and so on. We are never reminded to add something to our being, to our soul. If you just add this one ingredient, celebration, to your life, so much will be transformed. Enjoyment and celebration have to be cultivated, until they become a habit. This feeds the feeling state for the positive Law of Attraction. Laugh, dance, sing, smile, enjoy yourself. You can keep your life exactly the same, adding just one thing: celebration.

One of the ancient sources for this addition of celebration into our lives is the Eastern tradition of Tao. Here is the legend of the origins of Tao and an illustration of how this tradition has profound meaning for us now.

Celebrate the Path

Legend has it that the great Chinese mystic Lao Tzu was born laughing. Usually, children are born crying, so this is a remarkable fact. Everybody was shocked. His mother and father could not believe it. And he wasn't just smiling, he was *laughing*. And he remained a laugher all his life. He chose Chuang Tzu as his disciple and successor because Chuang Tzu constantly made people laugh. He created absurd stories and tickled people's funny bones.

Lao Tzu and his disciple created not an organized religion but an individual approach to enlightenment called Tao. And Tao means "the path" — no goal. There is no goal, only the path.

How can we incorporate this paradox of no goal, only the path, into our lives?

Tao states that our lives are successful when we incorporate in equal proportion the qualities of quietude and activity. An image Taoists often use is that of a great rooted tree (quietude) next to a flowing river (activity). If you like visualizing, close your eyes for a moment and visualize a great rooted tree on the banks of a flowing river. Or stand up, hold out your arms, and say out loud, "I lovingly hold and embrace all my experiences with ease and joy." The real essence of Tao teaches us how to turn the worst into the best, to find opportunities for festivity in every situation. We can have goals and enjoy the journey.

FOUR-MINUTE MEDITATION: *Balancing Quietude and Activity* ✪

BENEFITS

Quietude accesses your wisdom and creativity. Activity brings tangible results that have heart and meaning for you. Balance these two in your life. Ultimately you make choices that support and nurture the deepest core of who you are. Enjoy the path!

STEP ONE: QUIETUDE

Write down one of your goals. Then close your eyes and turn your focus to your present reality, which might be far from the goal. Savor where you are right now, allowing yourself to celebrate the current situation. If you notice complaining thoughts that this or that is not yet happening, let them go by with nonjudgment and compassion.

STEP TWO: ACTIVITY

Write down one activity that you can do today to bring you one step closer to your goal. Through wise choice you have the ability to select positive and abundant changes for yourself.

There is no division between our day-to-day activities and the sacred, which we access in quietude. It is one universe. The division is created only by having two outlooks. And the more joyous you are, the more full of juice, love, laughter, music, and dance you are, the more beautiful your journey becomes.

FOUR-MINUTE MEDITATION: *Celebrate Rejection* ✪

BENEFITS

This technique activates the Law of Attraction and keeps you in a positive feeling state. It builds self-confidence and trust in the wealth of creative resources within you.

This technique comes from the Zen tradition. The way of Zen is zigzag; it does not always seem logical. When you experience a rejection, small or big, celebrate! For example, your boyfriend dumped you, you got fired, your submission to a magazine was rejected. Even if it seems illogical, celebrate anyway. And trust that there is a golden lining in the dark cloud. It is there; it just might be temporarily obscured from sight.

MEDITATION: *Yes! Yes! Yes!*

BENEFITS

This easy, quick technique helps you stay in a positive mind-set and attract good things. It is powerful in its simplicity and flexibility because it can bring positive change for you in seconds.

This technique is very simple. Just say the word *yes!* out loud with all your heart, going deeper and deeper into the word. Do it now. Say yes to everything. Say yes to good and to bad, to day and to night, to success and to failure. Say yes to life and to death. Just remember that one word — *yes!* — particularly when something happens that you do not like or did not want to have happen.

Now I want to introduce to you a powerful expressive meditation technique that helps you travel deep into the heart of celebration. It entails a longer time commitment but rewards you with long-lasting results.

EXPRESSIVE MEDITATION: *Dancing*

BENEFITS

When you do this dancing meditation, you release a tremendous amount of tension, and creative insights arise. Tension is simply trapped energy. The wild and free movement of the dance is a great way to set this energy free and get it moving. Feeling free in your body allows your mind to expand, your heart to open, and your spirit to soar. Then, when you lie still immediately after dancing, your gross level of activity — the body — is stopped, and the energy you have released travels inward to the subtler layers of your being. This technique allows the dynamism of the dance to move to your roots, to the very core of your being, liberating great feelings of joy and positivity.

Do you ever put on your favorite dancing music when no one is around and just cut loose? It's a great way to release tension and unwind. With a few simple additions, this pleasurable experience can become a meditation.

Historically, Sufis have had a tradition of dancing as a meditation in celebration of life. The following dancing meditation, created by Indian mystic and teacher Osho, is called Osho Nataraj. You can find information about ordering the *Osho Nataraj* CD created for this meditation on p. 207. If you choose not to order the CD, I suggest doing this meditation to any inspiring and celebratory music you like, but keep to the same music every time you do this meditation. That way it is easier to notice how your experience of the meditation changes each time.

You can do this meditation any time of day. It takes about sixty-five minutes. (You can also do it for four minutes — two minutes of stage one and two minutes of stage two — or for any amount of time that you have. Just know that the deepest benefits come when you do the full sixty-five minutes.) Do this technique especially if you are having trouble coming to stillness when you meditate. Dancing into meditation is a great way to direct your energy inward.

STAGE ONE: DANCING (FORTY MINUTES)

Clear a space where you can dance safely with your eyes closed. Put on the *Osho Nataraj* CD or a CD of your own choosing. Close your eyes or cover them with a blindfold, and dance for forty minutes. Let go of any sense of control and disappear into the dance. Allow your body to respond to the music any way it likes, from wildly to very slowly and gently. Celebrate yourself. Become like a child again, in love with movement for its own sake. No one can see you, and this experience is not about performing or looking good, which always creates a subtle tension. If feelings arise, express them through the dance. You have complete freedom to do any movement you want.

Let the sense that you are *observing* yourself dance fall away naturally. You and the movement and the music are one. Dancing is no longer a *doing*, but a *happening*.

As you continue to dance, you may start to forget that you are dancing and to feel that you are the dance. Unlike those times when you are still aware of the separation between you and the dance, between you and the music, it becomes a meditation when the divisions dissolve and you are totally involved, totally merged into the dance. You do not need to do anything to force this shift; just allow it to happen.

STAGE TWO: STILLNESS (TWENTY MINUTES)

The next stage of the meditation is silent. Turn off the music and immediately lie down for twenty minutes. (It is okay to sit if you cannot lie down.) The *Osho Nataraj* CD includes this twenty minutes of silence, but if you don't have the CD, simply set a timer and, keeping your eyes closed, be totally silent and still.

STAGE THREE: GET UP AND DANCE AGAIN (FIVE MINUTES)

To complete the meditation, turn on the music again and dance for five minutes. Celebrate and enjoy your body and the sense of total freedom dancing like this gives you.

GRATITUDE

One of the most profound benefits I gained from inviting more laughter into my life was to experience gratitude for what I have. I became aware of a more subtle layer of myself that previously had gone undetected: the complaining mind. I had been taught to look at what I did not have, to focus on what was lacking in my life. As I allowed more laughter to fill me, my natural joy appeared, and my outlook started to change. I began to feel good for no reason and grateful for what I had. It seemed to happen as a by-product of laughter.

Being thankful, I discovered, is the highest form of thought. It contains a quality of wonder that can magnify our happiness. It lifts us out of the logical mind, which insists it knows what our lives are about, and into a realm of possibility, infinite magic, and mystery, where dreams really can come true. The impossible becomes possible. The logical mind can only plan out our lives based on past experiences. It doesn't have the capacity to imagine, to dream, to trust the mysterious unknown. Gratitude helps us access a place beyond the controlling mind where trust, creativity, and imagination reside.

As we live joyfully and contentedly, regardless of the situation, regardless of what we have or don't have, we discover that joy is not dependent on anything. It arises from within us. Gratitude fosters this state of being. We can, for example, become aware of what the universe is giving us every day: the sun rises and sets, the birds sing, the wind blows, flowers bloom. The moon and the stars come out at night. The universe goes on giving us all this and more, whether or not we are aware of it.

Do you take this for granted? Or do you notice?

Contentment and Desire

When you become aware you see, but if you are full of the clouds of complaining, then your vision is blocked. If your eyes are filled with smoke you cannot see the flame. Contentment is a different way of seeing life, in which you are not filtering what you see through your desires but seeing what is already there. Desire is like the horizon, always there somewhere in the future. When you see things out of your desire, you are in a state of discontent. And discontent is hell. Put aside your desire and just see. Then contentment envelops you, allowing you to see reality, what is, the good and the bad, and to embrace both.

MEDITATION: *Contentment*

STEP ONE

Contentment is your awareness of all that is already here. This awareness allows a tremendous gratitude and relaxation to arise. Desire impedes our ability to experience contentment and creates tension. But before we can lift ourselves out of our desires, we must be able to look them squarely in the eye. Write down one of your desires. Close your eyes and focus on it.

STEP TWO

Become more and more aware of your desire, and don't fight with it. Accept it. Then watch every step of the desire: how it arises, how it possesses you, how it drives you crazy, and then how it leaves you weak, frustrated, defeated. Watch the entire process, and that very watching brings freedom.

Once you have become perfectly aware of what desires are there, there's not much left to be done. Contentment arises within you. It was always there, just buried under the desires.

Effortless Effort

In the Zen tradition, there is no way or path; hence Zen practice is called the pathless path, the gateless gate, effortless effort, actionless action, or nondoing. Practitioners use these contradictory terms to point toward a certain truth: *a path means the goal has to be in the future, and you are here now.* Understanding the paradox is significant in understanding the spirit of Zen. This tradition teaches you both effort and effortlessness, because unless you attain effortless effort, which looks paradoxical, you have not attained. Zen says that you cannot arrive because you are already here.

Now that I've got you thoroughly confused, let's see how to make sense of this in your day-to-day life.

To allow effortless effort to manifest in your life may seem like a daunting task. And yet, if you reflect on past experiences, you probably recall many instances when your actions were spontaneous and natural, when they arose out of the needs of the moment without thought of profit or tangible result.

Effortless effort is a state in which the world seems to be working for you. It is based on relaxation and gratitude. Do you know what I mean? Can you think of a time when you felt calm yet alert and your actions were spontaneous, natural, and effortless? Expressions such as "going with the flow" and "swimming with the current" are often used to describe this state. Zen says that if a warrior is to succeed, success must come gently, with effort but no stress or obsession. The behavior arises from a relaxed sense of oneself as connected to others and to one's environment. It is not motivated by a sense of separateness, nor is it inertia, laziness, or passivity.

To understand how this works, we must be quiet and watchful, learning to listen to both our own inner voice and the voices of our environment in *a noninterfering, receptive manner*. In this way we also learn to rely on more than just our intellect and logical mind to gather and assess information. We develop and trust our intuition as our direct connection to ourselves and to our environment. We heed the intelligence of our whole body, not just our brain. And we *learn through our own experience*. All this allows us to respond readily to the needs of the environment, which of course includes us. This promotes more harmony and balance, not just for us but for everyone around us. Effortless effort simply flows through us because it is the right action, appropriate to its time and place, and serves the purpose of greater harmony and balance.

In this process we learn to trust our bodies, our thoughts, and our emotions and also to believe that the environment will provide support and guidance. You might already have experiences of this, when help has come to you from an unexpected source.

A fun way of practicing this principle is to *offer* help to people who would never expect it. Doing this helps to affirm your trust in the universe that the same can happen to you.

Detaching from the outcome and letting go of any hope of profit are key. We know intuitively that actions that are not ego motivated but are in response to the needs of the environment lead to harmonious balance and give meaning and purpose to our lives. Such actions are attuned to the deepest flow of life itself.

Timing is an important aspect of effortless effort. We can learn to perceive processes in their earliest stages and then to take timely action. For example, when it comes to our health, early diagnosis can save us from many difficulties. Or we can intuit that a certain conversation we need to have, if timed right, will produce the most creative result. Again, you probably already have had experiences of good (and bad!) timing.

By taking quiet time and listening carefully within, as well as to our surroundings, by remembering that we are part of an interconnected whole, *by remaining still until action is called forth*, we can perform valuable, necessary, and long-lasting service in the world while cultivating our ability to be at one with the flow.

This simple meditation is a great way to get the knack of effortless effort. It is deeply relaxing and helps us to access our inner wisdom and creativity.

Over time, as you get used to this practice, doing it every day if you can, you can experiment with ten, twenty, or thirty minutes. You can also apply the principles of effortless effort to your day-to-day activities, once you have gotten used to the feeling of it with this practice.

FOUR-MINUTE MEDITATION: *Effortless Effort*

STEP ONE

Choose a place that is relaxing for you: your living room, the porch, your local park. There is nothing to "do," no agenda, nothing to achieve, nowhere to go. You can start by sitting, standing up, or lying down — it doesn't matter.

STEP TWO

Think of one thing you are grateful for. Notice how you feel when you think about it. Now allow yourself to follow your intuition. You might do something, such as walking, dancing, or gazing at the trees, or you might do nothing. It doesn't matter. It is not the activity that is important but your relaxed, spontaneous, effortless effort with the activity or nonactivity. Over time you discover that you can do activities with a goal, such as cleaning the kitchen floor, but it feels effortless and relaxing, which adds to your enjoyment.

If you simply allow things to happen, not choosing, then you can deeply, respectfully, and gratefully accept whatever comes to you as a gift from the universe.

Search in the Right Direction

Ultimately there are no words to express gratitude. We just have to bow down in deep gratitude, in silence. A real prayer is non-verbal; words are inadequate. You may even find tears are rolling down your cheeks, or you may find yourself dancing with joy, singing, or laughing. You have had to renounce the word. Down through the ages this is the same conclusion that thousands of mystics have reached. And in that moment you become united with the whole of existence, the message of the wind blowing through the trees and the poetry of a bubbling brook. As language disappears, the mind is of no more use. You contact existence directly, without the mediation of the mind, and that experience is enlightenment. It is within everyone's reach. Even if it is only for a few moments to start with, over time the experience takes root and grows.

Every situation carries a hidden blessing. Granted, sometimes it's heavily disguised. If you can't see it, then pray for it to be revealed to you. Choosing to feel grateful for painful situations paves the way for peace of mind, prosperity, and joy in your day-to-day life.

⬥ FOUR-MINUTE MEDITATION: *Focus on the Good*

BENEFITS

As you make a practice of becoming habituated to focusing on the positive, you add to the number of good things in your life. Over time you start to attract more and more of these good things.

STEP ONE

Think of one positive thing in your life. However difficult it might be to think of good things, see if you can think of at least one. Be thankful for it. Feel yourself filled with warmth; feel your heart expand.

STEP TWO

As you access this feeling state of thankfulness, you are tuning in with a higher vibration. Now notice how the thankfulness deepens as you continue to focus on this good feeling state.

FOUR-MINUTE MEDITATION: *You Are Unique* ✦

BENEFIT

This technique helps you to like yourself, love yourself, and accept yourself. You are unique, and you have a unique purpose for being here. This becomes manifest the more you nourish and trust yourself.

STEP ONE

Focus on one thing you like about yourself. If it helps, write it down and/or say it out loud. For example: "_____ [your name here], you are kindhearted."

STEP TWO

Notice if thoughts of comparison come up and you start to think of yourself as higher or lower than another. Bring compassion and nonjudgment to this awareness. Feel grateful for who you are in this moment. It's not about being perfect. It's about being happy with who you are right now. Over time, add to the things you like about yourself.

CHILDREN

The birth of my son was a major turning point in my life, a defining moment that led to a decision. I knew that if I did not free myself from the straitjacket of anger, pain, and fear and find my authentic self, my son would suffer. He would be another person in a straitjacket, and the cycle would continue. I knew that I would transmit my uncomfortable emotions to him if I did not learn how to transform them into positive ones.

Have you ever experienced a defining moment in your life when suddenly the direction you had to take became crystal clear?

I chose to respond to this wake-up call because I did not want to put my son through what I had been through as a child. Nor did I want to wake up one day when he was eighteen years old and be full of regrets.

Children are mirrors. We can shut them down because we don't want to look in the mirror, or we can use the mirror as a tool for transformation. I chose to look in the mirror because I saw the opportunity I was being given. A child is a gift. I wanted to do the best I could for him and for myself. Was it always easy? No, but I knew that my son's presence in my life was helping me peel away the layers of frenzy and noise that had accumulated inside me, bringing me to the stillness that was awaiting me — the stillness that is me.

My son's innocence, trust, joy, and laughter mirrored to me that I had lost touch with these qualities in myself. My own "inner child" was lost, shut down. I could now invite her back to relive all those times again. Just because I was an adult didn't mean I couldn't *now* play, laugh, sing, dance, watch Walt Disney movies, and do all the things I had missed out on in my childhood. Suddenly life was fun again, full of infinite possibilities, as I realized I could give myself, and my son, permission to allow the qualities of wonder, spontaneity, imagination, and creativity to be expressed.

The first social activity a child expresses is smiling, a natural and spontaneous way to connect. The parents are thrilled — I certainly was. When a child smiles, it means she loves and is happy. Other things come later, but a smile is the first joyful sign of being in the world. And we can all keep smiling our whole lives!

Children love to laugh, dance, sing, play, and learn. They are closer to meditation because they have had less conditioning. They are closer to their true authentic selves. And they love to have quiet time.

Children need to have a form of meditation in their lives as much as us grown-ups do. My experience has been that the expressive techniques in this book are ideally suited to children. They are already laughing and playing. Just offer them a quiet few minutes to sit or lie down after their activity. This will help them calm down, for example, before eating or before going to bed or before a math test!

CHILDREN'S TWO-MINUTE EXPRESSIVE MEDITATION:
Laughter *

BENEFITS

The first step helps children — and you as well — to release a lot of tension, and the second step brings centering and grounding. Try this meditation with your children. Vary the length of time depending on the ages, personalities, and schedule you have to work with. Be creative.

STEP ONE: LAUGHTER

You and the children shout "yahoo!" three times, and then burst out laughing. Try it for one or two minutes. (For more details, see p. 9.)

STEP TWO: SITTING OR LYING DOWN IN SILENCE

Ring a chime or bell (better than shouting out "stop," which can be jarring) and have the kids sit or lie down quietly for one or two minutes. The more you do this with them, the more they will get into the rhythm and idea of it, and you might be able to try four minutes of each step, depending on your situation.

Always allow the same amount of time for each step. Allow the children to continue to laugh in the silent step until the laughter naturally dies down. Just make sure they have their eyes closed for the second step.

Every child is born a buddha. Every adult is born a child, is born a buddha. What do I mean by a "buddha"? I mean someone with a silent mind and a heart full of love and trust, innocence, spontaneity, authenticity, and laughter. And an innate wisdom that comes not from knowledge but from the heart.

Did you know that children laugh on average between three hundred and three hundred fifty times a day, and adults only ten to fifteen times a day? When did we decide that life is such a grim affair?

✳ MORE CHILDREN'S TWO-MINUTE EXPRESSIVE MEDITATIONS

GIBBERISH: Good for expressing anger and frustration and also for having fun (see p. 65).

DANCING: Good for unleashing creativity, activating joy, and releasing tension (see p. 28).

HUMMING: Good for healing the heart and for centering (see p. 132).

THE CHILDREN'S MYSTIC ROSE MEDITATION: Good for laughter, tears, and silence (see p. 50).

RUNNING: Good for releasing tension and activating life energy and joy (see p. 184).

PLAYING: Good on every level.

DRAWING/PAINTING/CRAYONING: Good for creativity, relaxation, fun.

Follow the same directions as for the Children's Laughter meditation. The first expressive step is always to be followed by approximately the same amount of sitting or lying down in silence — or being as quiet as the children can be. My experience is that sometimes children need more time to let off steam, and so it might take them a little longer to fall into a collective quiet. Allow them to find it themselves without being authoritative or judging them. Keep it short, unless *they* ask for it to be longer (which they might well do). Make it fun, light, a sharing. Introduce them to the principles of nonjudgment of themselves and others, of compassion for themselves and others, of relaxation, and of witnessing. Do not use force. If they don't want to do it, let go of the idea. Suggest it at another time. If the word *meditation* is not appropriate to use in your situation, call these "relaxation techniques," "fun time," or other words of your choice.

FOR PARENTS

Do the Laughter meditation as a family. Or choose the Gibberish meditation, or whichever ones most appeal to you. My son's favorites were the Laughter and the Gibberish. Your kids will respond to your respect, love, and gratitude with deeper respect, more gratitude, more love. There is no "generation gap" if you respect and are friendly to your children.

Our children come through us. We do not own them. They are an expression of Life's longing to continue itself. We give them love, a home, and support, but we must not impose our thoughts and ambitions on them. Their souls have a purpose for their future, and it is not for us to interfere. Our purpose as parents is to send them forth into the world full of confidence in their true authentic selves, knowing that not only can they lead happy, productive lives but also that they can bring much good to others.

MARY POPPINS

I was first introduced to the movie *Mary Poppins* when I took my son and his friends to see it. Like many parents, I suppose, I got used to taking the kids to Walt Disney and similar movies, without thinking much about the effect they were having on me. It was when my son became a teenager that I realized I missed fun, uplifting children's movies such as *Mary Poppins*. Why was that?

I discovered that *Mary Poppins,* as just one example, reminds me of the infinite possibilities that become available to us when we go beyond the rational, controlling mind. The father in the movie, Mr. Banks, believes that life is all work and no play. His life is controlled by a strict schedule and a rigid way of looking at life and people. For example, he believes that children should be seen and not heard and that women should obey their husbands. Mrs. Banks, although attempting to free herself by attending suffragette meetings, is too afraid to stand up to her husband and speak her truth. It's the children who break free by writing a letter requesting a new nanny who is fun, plays games, and is kind. Mary Poppins magically shows up at the door. Suddenly there is a lot of singing, dancing, and laughing in the house, and even the birds join in. She teaches the children that an activity can be either fun or not, depending on your point of view. There is an element of fun in everything they do, even chores.

You find the fun, and snap, the job becomes a game. Try doing housework, raking the yard, or taking out the trash while singing, whistling, skipping, or dancing. Here's a practice to help get you started.

⭐ FOUR-MINUTE MEDITATION: *Snap! The Job's a Game*

STEP ONE

Choose a job that you do around the house, for example, vacuuming, unloading the dishwasher, taking out the trash. Notice your attitude to this job. Do you see it as a drag, something to get through in a hurry? Do you give it your total presence? Bring compassion and nonjudgment to whatever you discover about your attitudes.

STEP TWO

Snap your fingers. Now do the activity as if it were the most fun thing in the world. Sing, skip, whistle, dance — whatever it takes for you to turn this "chore" into a fun activity. As you make a practice of this, you get the knack of it and can apply it to other areas of your life. This technique works well with encouraging kids to tidy up their rooms!

My favorite scene in *Mary Poppins* is the visit with Uncle Albert, who can't stop laughing and, carried away by his own mirth, rises up to the ceiling. The infectious laughter eventually has the whole tea party up on the ceiling. On the surface this might seem a fanciful story for children, but the energy of laughter really does help us rise up, okay, maybe not up to the ceiling, but to feeling positive, on top of the world, as if anything is possible. The important thing is how it makes us *feel*. Have you ever felt that way when laughing, that suddenly life is good, that you can achieve great things?

Mr. Banks describes life as a looming battle to be faced and fought. Is that what you were taught about life? I know I was.

Gradually the infectiousness of Mary Poppins and the children's positive energy seep through the walls of their father's mind-set. He pops out of it like a jack-in-the-box, suddenly released from the constraints of seriousness. He starts singing and dancing, flying kites, and laughing. A promotion at the bank is his reward, and everyone benefits. Mrs. Banks is freed from her fear, and the whole family flies kites in the park and enjoys fun and loving times together. Mary Poppins knows her work with this family is done and departs to help other children show their parents the creative power of laughter, fun, and play.

This story is a powerful account of how laughter and a positive attitude can shift your mind-set and create a more joyful, creative, and prosperous life. Who do you relate to in this movie? The children? The father? The mother? Or Mary Poppins?

You can reap enormous benefits if you practice these laughter techniques. The magic is that things can happen even when you're not looking for them to, as long as you keep your eyes open and stay alert. If you are ready and open, you see the opportunity and seize it.

Enhance Your Creativity

Do you feel like you are stuck in a box like Mr. Banks? How can you discover where your creativity lies? I used to think that creativity had to be expressed in activities such as painting, drawing, and doing pottery, for example. I love playing tennis, reading, listening to music, dancing, singing, seeing movies, and traveling, but I didn't used to think of these as creative.

As I followed these passions, my authentic self started emerging. These activities filled me with joy, and they do to this day. *Creativity is the quality that you bring to whatever activity you are doing*; it is an attitude, an inner approach — how you look at things, exactly as Mary Poppins describes. It has nothing to do with the activity in particular. What matters is your attitude toward it. You can cook in a creative or an uncreative way — it all depends on you. Some people turn into master chefs, others open a can of soup for dinner. But then maybe the master chef is a terrible dancer and the can-of-soup person dances magically. It doesn't matter what we are passionate about — what matters is that we follow our passion, allowing our creativity to arise from that. Every child is creative. Children are so in the moment, so in touch with their innate joy, and spending time with children can greatly enhance your own creativity.

Whatever you do, if you do it joyfully and lovingly, and not purely out of economic motives, then it is creative. Love what you do, regardless of what it is. If you clean the floor with love, you have created beauty in that clean floor. You have lived these moments in such delight that they have promoted your inner growth. You cannot be the same after a creative act. Its value is intrinsic. Seemingly small things become great when touched with love and delight.

To be creative is to be close to the divine, but this closeness is available only to those who pour their whole energy into it. Discover your innermost joy and passion, and do it. Make what is invisible inside you visible, make the dream exist on the earth, let the dream become actual. Transform the potential into the actual: this is the greatest joy there is. You attain real bliss when you have helped the divine shine through, when you have made the world a little more beautiful, when you have enhanced its joy. Live at your optimum. Don't think of life as a burden, a duty to be fulfilled. Make it a dance; let it be a celebration.

You were a child once. As you pay attention to magical moments from your childhood, you help your creativity, passion, and joy grow. A new life energy runs through you. You become more receptive, more loving.

| FOUR-MINUTE MEDITATION: *Gather Moments of Joy* ⚙ |

STEP ONE

Remember one moment from your childhood, from joyful times, when you felt that life was magic, that just to be alive was ecstatic, that just to breathe was enough. You didn't need anything to make you joyful. Gather this moment. Close your eyes and remember it.

STEP TWO

Now relive this moment. Become a child again. Run, sing, play. As you continue this practice, do it for a longer time, ten, twenty, or thirty minutes. If memories are triggered of times your passion for a particular activity was cut off, reinfuse that activity with passion now. Your life becomes revitalized with creativity and joy.

Find Your Inner Mary Poppins

Creativity is the ability to see what other people can't. How can we be creative when our sight is clouded by an overbusy mind? Spending time doing nothing, relaxing, walking in nature, sitting on your porch, enjoying any kind of downtime that you can fit into your day: all these help you tune in to your creativity. The Laughter (p. 9) and Dancing (p. 28) meditations help. Having fun, being playful, playing sports and games, singing and dancing, and whistling all enhance our creative process. Laughter breaks up the serious grip of the mind so that our natural talents can shine through.

LAUGHTER AND TEARS:
THE OSHO MYSTIC ROSE MEDITATION

Laughter and tears may look contradictory, but they are not. Laughing and crying are deeply related; they are two sides of the same energy. In certain situations you can either burst out laughing or burst into tears. Both help relieve tension. Whenever we are overwhelmed with something, we either cry or laugh. If we laugh for a long time, tears come. If we go on crying, we will suddenly start to laugh.

A rainbow appears when the sun and rain appear at the same time. They both nourish the soil; both are needed. The same is true of laughter and tears. *Our spiritual nurturing is fed by the sunshine of our laughter and the rain of our tears.* This combination brings the greatest happiness and peace we could wish for.

If you feel like laughing, laugh; if you feel like crying, cry. The tears that you hold in weigh down your being. The laughter that you miss is a weight on your soul. Whatever happens in the moment, give it expression. This is how you can transcend anything that threatens to pull you away from the purity of your love. This is how you claim your dignity as a human being and feel self-respect as a part of this beautiful universe. Love creates a spiritual equality, and laughter and tears create a spiritual equality as well. By spiritual equality I mean realizing you are just as valued by the universe as the smallest blade of grass, the tallest mountain, the wealthiest and most famous people. Love, laughter, and tears bring us together in divine harmony.

The Mystic Rose meditation is longer and more powerful than any of the shorter techniques, and it takes you into a deeper place inside yourself. It requires a greater commitment, not just of your time but of your willingness to dig deep within yourself. The benefits are also much longer lasting and, since they are more deeply rooted within you, bring a profound transformation on the emotional, physical, and mental levels.

This technique was created by Osho as the second in a series of what he called "meditative therapies." Because many of us have lost the capacity to sit in silence, these techniques were developed to work as a bridge, to clear the ground for deeper meditation. They are perfect for handling the pressures of our twenty-first-century lifestyle, designed, as they are, to release us from years of repressed emotions, of physical tension in the body, and of old ideas and beliefs that no longer work for us. So much energy is tied up in unexpressed emotion. By letting the feelings out, we can go into deeper and deeper layers, releasing and healing.

The Mystic Rose meditation is a three-week process of three hours each day. The first week is for laughter, for expressing our natural joy and love of life. Spending a week in laughter is a great way to open up more to our feelings. The second week is for crying, for a deep healing and unburdening of the heart. After releasing pent-up emotions through crying, we are ready to simply sit and observe, the core of meditation. The third week, which Osho called "the watcher on the hills," is for sitting silently in deep meditation. It brings about an integration, a closure.

Since you are probably just recovering from the shock of reading, in the previous paragraph, about doing this practice for three hours a day for three weeks, let me say here that you can start this technique alone or with a friend(s) with two minutes a day, or however much time you have.

You can find information on where you can participate in this meditation on my website, www.pragito.com, or at www.osho.com.

EXPRESSIVE MEDITATION: *The Osho Mystic Rose*

Devote the same amount of time to each stage, and do the stages in sequence: laughing, crying, watching. Remember, however, that you reap the most powerful benefits when you do three hours each day for three weeks. I do understand that this is a tall order for some of you who have a full-time job and/or kids. If this is the case, start with two minutes a day, as I mentioned above. There is also a Children's Mystic Rose, which takes one hour a day for three weeks. See pp. 39–41, where I make suggestions for meditations involving children.

STAGE ONE: LAUGHTER MEDITATION (SEE P. 9)

To laugh for three hours for no reason is an extraordinary experience. I still remember the first time I did the Mystic Rose. I was so worried that I wouldn't be able to laugh, especially for so long. I had even been secretly hoping, before I signed up, that the three weeks would not fit with my schedule. But it fit perfectly! I had enough time left over in my vacation to complete the process before returning home. The universe took care of my excuses! After a week, you find you have shed many layers of tension and that you are more relaxed. You feel energized, full of aliveness and positivity. You discover a greater awareness of the comedy of life and a new sense of humor about yourself.

STAGE TWO: CRYING (SEE PP. 83–84)

In *Crying: The Mystery of Tears*, Dr. William H. Frey said, "The reason people feel better after crying is that they may be removing, in tears, chemicals that build up during emotional stress. Emotional tears have a chemically different content from irritant-induced tears like the ones that appear when we slice onions. Something unique is happening when we cry emotional tears. When we use the expression 'to cry it out,' that literally may be true. People do feel better after crying."

As I've said, both laughter and crying release emotional tension; they are two sides of the same coin, but in the Mystic Rose we start with laughter because it is easier to laugh than to cry. Laughter prepares us to open up; it helps us to move into our hearts so that by day eight we are very ready to cry and to feel. Then, after seven days of crying, we feel cleansed, opened, and deeply relaxed, ready to move into the last stage, where we will integrate the processes of laughing and crying.

STAGE THREE: THE WATCHER ON THE HILLS (SEE P. 142)
This last stage serves as a centering meditation, after all the expression and emotional release. A lot of space has been opened up in you in the past two weeks, and you now have an even greater capacity for silence, peace, and spiritual nurturing.

The watcher on the hills is about awareness, focus, and staying awake. You don't do anything, you just relax, but this is an alert relaxation. In this week, you are practicing disidentification — the capacity to step back and watch. Let yourself be with the moment, and watch whatever is happening. Thoughts, feelings, body movements, outside noises: allow them all, without judgment, to be a part of your awareness.

We are not used to doing nothing. This meditation is a way to help us move from doing to being, from outward to inward. If you become aware that you've spaced out or gotten lost in your thoughts, simply come back to the present moment and go back to watching. No judgments, no comparisons, no goal. Simply be.

The first time I did the watcher on the hills was also the first time that I sat in a silent meditation for any length of time. Believe me, the thought of being just with my mind for three hours a day for a week was not an exciting prospect. But, as is so often the case, the reality was a pleasant surprise. I actually found it rather easy to sit and just absorb the changes and insights I'd had over the previous two weeks. The point here is not to close off the mind — in fact, my mind was very active — but to learn to watch it and to develop the awareness that we are not, in fact, the same as our minds. We can simply observe what goes on in the mind as if from a distance.

Once we reach that place of watcher or witness or observer, we suddenly see ourselves with more clarity and objectivity. We can look at all the dramas in our lives with perspective and compassion.

Think of this as gardening, as taking care of the flowers (intuition and inner wisdom) in our inner gardens. In order to nurture the seedlings we must be watchful of weeds (negative, fearful thoughts and judgments) so that the flowers can come to full bloom. We must also be watchful of intruders (others who might be verbally or physically abusive to us) who might crush and destroy the flowers. When the gardener is home (watching, observing, but not judging) the flowers are safe and can blossom, offering their beauty and fragrance to whoever passes by.

Becoming a watcher on the hills frees us from the supremacy of the mind. It allows our inner wisdom full expression, which then creates the very opening we need for the insight and perspective to create our lives just the way we want them to be.

ADDITIONAL MEDITATIONS FOR LAUGHTER

FOUR-MINUTE MEDITATION: *The Law of Attraction*

BENEFITS

By transmitting vibrations of wealth and abundance, you are attracting like vibrations. The more you do this, the more you create what you want and the more you trust that what is meant for you is coming to you.

STEP ONE

The Law of Attraction states that like attracts like. Choose one occasion from your past when you felt filled with joy. Relive that memory. Feel the joy inside you now. This is helping you create the *feeling state* of the positive Law of Attraction.

STEP TWO

Now give thanks, with your full and abundant heart, for everything that you have right now. Feel your inner wealth.

FOUR-MINUTE MEDITATION: *Paradise Now*

BENEFITS

If you can't enjoy yourself, you cannot help others to enjoy themselves. If you are not really contented with yourself, you cannot help others to attain contentment. Enjoy yourself, be bliss filled. And when you are overflowing with your own bliss, that bliss reaches others as well.

Paradise is nothing but the capacity to enjoy yourself right here and now. When you are alone, enjoy yourself; when you are with others, enjoy love and friendship. You are free to enjoy each moment in your totality. If something inside you is impeding your joy, observe it, with compassion and nonjudgment. When you live in self-condemnation, you live in hell. When you accept yourself and you enjoy yourself, you are in heaven. Why not do this now?

⚙ FOUR-MINUTE MEDITATION: *Inner Smile*

BENEFITS

Once you have smiled in this way, you may remain happy for twenty-four hours. Whenever you feel that you are missing that happiness, just close your eyes and catch hold of that smile again. In the daytime, as many times as you want, you can catch hold of it. It is always there.

Do this *now*.

Sitting down, relax the lower jaw and open the mouth slightly. Start breathing from the mouth, but not deeply. Just let the body breathe so that your breathing is shallow and becomes more and more shallow.

Your whole body will feel very relaxed. Start feeling a smile — not on your face but all over your inner being. This is not a smile that comes to the lips; it is an inner smile, an existential smile.

Do this meditation when you go to bed, or at any time. It is as if you are smiling from the belly. It is a smile, not laughter, so it is very soft, delicate, and fragile, like a small flower opening in the belly, its fragrance spreading over the body.

FOUR-MINUTE MEDITATION: *Prosperity* ⚙

BENEFITS

> *The more we radiate our wholeness outward, the more we attract prosperity on every level: financially, emotionally, spiritually.*

Gratitude is the secret. Take a few moments to sit down, close your eyes, and feel everything you are grateful for. The emphasis here is on the word *feel*. In the feeling state of gratitude, we are full and whole. Then radiate that wholeness so that everyone can be touched by it.

Look for something to be grateful for, even in the most difficult situations.

PART TWO

Tears

After spending so much time in laughter, we inevitably come to tears, the polar opposite expression of energy. Life is comedy and tragedy. Understanding and allowing our tears, as well as our laughter, reaps rich rewards. Tears express the inexpressible. Whenever our innermost cup of emotion becomes too full — of happiness, sadness, or anything else — it overflows as tears.

Just as thoughts are the language of the mind, tears are the language of the heart. If the heart has become frozen, tears signal the beginning of the thaw. The more we allow tears, the more our heart melts. When tears come like a flood, we need to learn not to judge them, because with their flowing, our heart starts to warm up, becomes alive. And as we thaw the garden of our heart, love begins to grow like a flower.

Tears are also like prayer, cleansing our spiritual vision. We shouldn't try to interpret or analyze our tears. Words are inadequate for conveying their meaning. If we simply allow our tears, we become one with ourselves, with our heart.

My intention in this second part of the book is to demonstrate that you can meditate from a painful place, just as you can from a joyful place, as discussed in part 1. You can be wherever you are emotionally and still be in meditation. You do not have to be happy all the time. Sorrow also has its place of beauty and divinity.

Darkness belongs to God just as light does; the night is just as beautiful as the day. Compassion for ourselves is important, as is forgiveness, of ourselves and of others. What this means is that instead of repressing our pain we can embrace it, befriend it, and heal it.

Most people are aware of only the first dimension of tears — that of pain, suffering, misery, and sadness. When we are present with these feelings, we allow them to heal and transform into love, wisdom, and emotional stillness. For it is pain that can take us into a deeper place within ourselves and that can ultimately lead us to compassion, the highest form of love. Yet tears have a second dimension as well — they can be products of joy and ecstatic happiness. Have you ever cried out of joy, at your wedding or at your child's graduation, for example? These tears increase our happiness. The third dimension, the rarest one, is that of gratitude. This dimension comes to people who reach a place of deep connection to this whole beautiful universe, to the beauty of life itself and all the bounty that nature showers on us.

Tears are not rational. It is the mind that wants to have a rational, logical explanation for everything. So what can the mind do when the tears come? It has to learn to be nonjudgmental and compassionate and to allow the tears, even if there is absolutely no reason for them. Over time, letting the tears come helps us be more calm, relaxed, and at peace with ourselves.

Control is based on fear. When we are constantly trying to control everything, a great tension builds up in us. This tension can create pain and disease in the body and also the possibility of a sudden explosion of emotion when we least expect it. The more we understand ourselves, the inner workings of our body and mind, the easier it becomes to experience inner peace and the more the mind and the body work together in harmony.

Tears are beneficial. On the physical level they help the eyes see more clearly, and on the spiritual level they give us more clarity of mind and access to our wisdom. Many people, particularly men, are told not to cry, because crying is seen as weakness. But tears should not be controlled, because they are cleansing. Even if they are tears of sadness, they take away our sadness and leave us calmer and quieter. If they are tears of happiness, they increase our happiness. And tears of gratitude cleanse our hearts and minds and make us feel fresh and new.

It is unfortunate that millions of people have never known the deepest aspects of tears. They know only the superficial, the ordinary. In their minds tears have become associated with pain, misery, anguish, and anxiety, and they remain unaware that tears can also become an expression of overwhelming blessings. If you have not known your tears as a benediction, you have missed out on a most beautiful experience of life.

When you learn to accept the more difficult feelings of grief, jealousy, disappointment, and fear, you find that you can *use* the energies of these feelings to take you deeper into wisdom and inner stillness. Acceptance is key, because if we do not accept our difficult feelings, we create more pain by fighting them. The kindest and gentlest way to manage pain is to accept it, to be with it, and in time it transforms into love.

I have reaped great benefits from the meditation techniques included here, and I hope you will too. Some are easier to do with friends. However, you can also do them alone; they are equally powerful either way. Just choose the ones you feel like doing. No one technique is better than another. All of them are designed to assist you in reaching your inner silence, peace, and joy.

STILL WATERS RUN DEEP:
EMOTIONAL CLEARING

My childhood experiences left me confused. Over time I came to live in a kind of paralyzed numbness, too terrified almost to be. So I developed two strategies: the first one was being silent, and the second was filling my life with noise.

My first idea was to keep my mouth shut and speak only when spoken to. This silence was based on fear, on swallowing my truth, my joy, my creative expression, as well as my anger and pain. This silence was the lid on a cauldron of mixed emotions; it was like a dormant volcano, which appears quiet and serene on the surface but can erupt at any moment.

Because I had no one to share my feelings with, I was lonely in my self-imposed silent exile. I had no idea that I was cutting myself off from the love that was available to me from others. The only people I felt safe and comfortable with were the characters of the books that I loved to read, and my cat.

The silence I created was also filled with self-judgment. I was constantly trying to figure out how to make my mother happy, trying to make sense of it all. What could be keeping her from taking responsibility, from showing sensitivity, from controlling her emotions? If I tried to talk to my father about it, he always replied, "There's nothing wrong with your mother!" I concluded, therefore, that everything was my fault, that there must be something wrong with me. If only I could be a better kid, I thought, then my mother would love me and treat me with more kindness.

It was only later, through the techniques described in this book, that I was able to heal and free myself from this silent bondage and find a natural inner silence filled with love, peace, and wisdom.

As I headed into my teenage years, I tried a different strategy: noise. I filled my life with partying, smoking, and drinking. I left home and went to college, where I was free at last, or so I thought.

Although I was physically free, I was not free inside. I felt rebellious, unhappy, and trapped. My first year in college I partied and drank myself into oblivion. I spent a lot of time with my head hung over the toilet, swearing to myself that I would never drink another drop of alcohol. But at the next party, there I was, armed with a cigarette in one hand and a drink in the other. I was incapable of having social interactions without my twin allies. My self-confidence depended on them.

This strategy was brought into sharp relief one morning when I woke up to find myself in bed with a guy I didn't know. I couldn't remember how I had met him or what had happened the night before. It was a pivotal moment in my life, and I made the decision to seek help and transform myself.

Later on, through the techniques described in this book, I learned how to express myself in a meditation context so that I could release all the emotional turmoil. The smoking, drinking, and promiscuity dropped away, and I was able to enjoy parties and socializing in a natural, balanced way.

The Search for Happiness

I wanted to be happy — really happy, not a fake, covering-over-emotional-turmoil happy. From my mother I had learned violence, bitterness, and rage; from my father I had learned love as power-lessness and denial of truth. How could I come to terms with those paradoxical lessons? I had to take control of my life to discover the truth. Vacillating between extreme isolation and wild partying was not the answer. The Beatles sang, "All you need is love." "Love is the answer," sang John Lennon. I agreed with him, but where could I find love? When would I be happy?

I started searching and heard about a whole range of medita-tion techniques, including a series of cutting-edge expressive tech-niques created by the spiritual teacher Osho. As I practiced these techniques I discovered who I was underneath the numbness, the pain, and the rage that had piled up, layer upon layer, within me over the years, and that had been covered over with large dollops of noise and distraction.

I discovered that our core of inner silence is the source of our power. When we have that, no one can manipulate us, dominate us, or use us in any way. From that place of silence within, we know our truth and are able to live by it. But when we lose access to our silence, we can so easily become confused, especially when we're hit with a wave of strong emotion. We become like a ship without an anchor, tossed around at the mercy of the elements.

Befriending Emotions for Transformation

Below are a range of suggestions and techniques that have helped me release and transform my more uncomfortable emotions. These practices and techniques help us accept, befriend, and ex-press the full range of our emotions — anger, frustration, joy, sad-ness, disappointment, excitement — and this leads us to the still, deep waters within. I invite you to read through the techniques slowly and start where you feel would be the best place. You may prefer the shorter ones, or you may find the longer ones to be of more benefit. What matters is that you find the techniques that work best for you, depending on your situation.

Identifying Feelings

The first step is to bring awareness to what you are feeling at any given moment. Here's a simple practice you can do: simply stop for thirty seconds and see if you can identify how you are feeling. Allow the feeling, whatever it is. Don't judge it. Whether you are numb or happy or sad or depressed, simply identify the feeling and accept it. There is never any right or wrong way to feel. Perhaps you're confused about what you're feeling or just don't know. Let that be okay too.

It's not always so easy to identify what we're feeling. Sometimes we don't want certain feelings to arise, even though they are undeniably there. Or we might judge ourselves, thinking we shouldn't be feeling this way or that.

It is vital that we start by bringing awareness to our feelings, because this allows us to see how affected we are by our moods. When we're in a good mood, everything looks good, and we tend to think and act clearly as a result. A low mood, however, often makes us reactive; it compromises our common sense and makes it harder for us to think and act clearly. The awareness itself can help us make allowances for the fact that we are low. We might, for instance, be extra loving with ourselves or drive more carefully. Tuning into ourselves also brings us greater awareness of and compassion for others.

Expressing, Releasing, and Transforming Feelings

Once you've identified what you're feeling, the next step is to express it. Unexpressed emotion ties up so much of our energy. The energy of the emotion actually lodges in our body as a stressor. By letting the feelings out, releasing all the disturbance, we can listen to our silence more easily. And this listening, in turn, relaxes us and clears the way for making good decisions, taking a particular course of action, or relating better with another person.

Transforming Anger into Creativity

Anger — and with it I include frustration, irritation, annoyance, and depression — is one of the most difficult emotions to work with. It clouds our good judgment; its noise obliterates our creativity, wisdom, and clarity of mind. When anger goes unexpressed, it often turns to depression (it is often said that depression is anger turned inward). Unexpressed anger creates a stagnation of energy, a blocked, heavy feeling of inertia, and we are finding increasing evidence that this blocked energy has a direct impact on our physical health.

For example, if it stays lodged in your body, your anger can do serious damage to your coronary arteries. A new study at Harvard Medical School and Deaconess Hospital, led by epidemiologist Murray A. Mittleman, MD, shows that outbursts of moderate to extreme anger heighten your risk of a heart attack. Moreover, the study reveals that the increased peril lingers for a couple of hours, even if the eruption of temper lasts for just a few minutes. According to Mittleman, the average risk of heart attack more than doubles in the two hours following an outburst of moderate or greater anger. The solution to this situation that I offer here is the expressive meditation called Gibberish. Designed to give us a safe outlet for our anger, this technique helps us avoid outbursts, as described above, which threaten our health. We can also discover what is underneath the anger, which is usually one of three things: hurt, fear, or unmet needs.

EXPRESSIVE MEDITATION: *Gibberish* ◎

BENEFITS

The Gibberish meditation helps us release poisons from our body and mind, which is good for our health. It offers an alternative to dumping our anger and frustrations on another individual, thus avoiding a destructive chain reaction. It also offers an alternative to repressing emotions through self-destructive habits such as overeating, substance abuse, and so on. We can learn to use the energy of anger and transform it into creativity, love, and joy. We can also transform victimhood into empowerment, thus freeing ourselves from mental/emotional prisons. Other emotions, such as joy, excitement, sadness, and grief — indeed, our full spectrum of emotions — can also be expressed with this technique, resulting in emotional balance, calm, and inner peace.

This technique comes from the Sufi tradition and was first introduced hundreds of years ago by a Sufi mystic named Jabbar. Start with two minutes for each stage. As you get used to it you can increase the amount of time to ten, twenty, or thirty minutes. Just be sure to spend equal time on stages one and two.

STAGE ONE

Close your eyes. Put on a blindfold if you can, because this helps keep the eyes closed. Start speaking in gibberish, any nonsense sounds. Don't worry about what you sound like. Make any sounds you like; just don't speak in a language or use words that you know. Allow yourself to express whatever needs to be expressed within you. Just go totally mad. This is therapeutic madness. Sing, cry, shout, scream, mumble. Let your body go free: stamp, stomp, jump, skip, lie down, run in circles. Do whatever you feel like doing without harming anyone. Do not let up. Keep a steady stream of sound going. If you are doing this meditation with other people, don't get distracted by what they are doing. Stay with what is happening with you. If you cannot make loud sounds, for example, if you live in an apartment complex, then mouth the sounds silently but with the same force as if you were shouting out loud.

STAGE TWO

Sit in silence and watch with nonjudgment. For more information on witnessing, see p. 142.

An experience I once had taught me how to transform anger into creativity. One hot August afternoon I was having an altercation with one of my neighbors about the parking situation on our street. He was angry that one of my friends had parked her car in his "territory." When I got home, I festered over our conversation, aware that my eight-year-old son would return soon from his Cub Scout outing. I did not want to run the risk of dumping my anger onto him; I had experienced too much displaced anger myself as a child. I had been practicing the Gibberish meditation technique for quite a few years to clear the backlog of anger, rage, and frustration that had accumulated in me from childhood. I was now aware that I needed to release my bottled-up feelings once again.

First I put on a blindfold, then I turned on my *Gibberish* CD (see p. 206). I stomped and hollered and ranted and raved against my neighbor — all in gibberish, of course! Aaah! It felt so good to release the hot anger from my body and mind, to take the lid off the pressure cooker. I felt like a dormant volcano that had been muttering and grumbling underground and then had exploded to get rid of all the unwanted garbage within. The meditation was a cleansing, a dumping out of emotional and mental poisons. After a while I noticed that the emotional charge of my anger was disappearing and that my sense of humor was returning. I found myself clowning around, mimicking my neighbor in gibberish, and generally laughing and guffawing at myself too. Suddenly I heard "stop" shouted from the CD.

I immediately stopped the gibberish and listened. The silence was profound. I then sat down for the second stage of this meditation technique, which is sitting in silence. I sat and watched: thoughts, feelings, and emotions. I felt a delicious silence descend upon me. Compassion for myself and my neighbor arose.

The hot anger inside me had transformed into cool compassion, because I'd *used* the energy of the anger to move me into compassion. As I sat in silence, my emotions were now calm; I could see the situation with more clarity. What a relief to be back home in integrity with myself! In addition, a possible solution arose in my mind. I returned to speak to my neighbor about the parking situation. He was receptive to my new idea, and we resolved to treat each other with friendliness and respect in the future. We were even able to joke about how upset we had become.

Empowering Victims and Bullies

Most people do one of two things with their anger. One option is to repress it. Women, for example, are taught that it is not ladylike to get angry (I certainly was taught that!). As a result, we become afraid of anger, our own or someone else's, and become paralyzed with fear rather than being able to respond to a situation. We become victims.

Alternatively, we dump our anger on someone else. In general, this option is a more masculine characteristic. We become bullies. Victims and bullies are trapped by their own unconscious. Victims internalize their anger, and bullies externalize it.

If we are a victim and have become paralyzed with fear, the

Gibberish meditation technique can help us get in touch with our anger, and we can learn to defend ourselves and create boundaries. Bullies can learn to redirect their anger into a safe context. Both victims and bullies then learn how anger transforms into love. Both become empowered, freed from an unconscious habit.

Anger in itself is not bad. But to hold onto and accumulate it is dangerous. If we hold it in for too long, it can explode to such an uncontrollable degree that we even risk dying—either having a heart attack or being angry enough to kill someone else. A person who can be totally angry can also be totally happy, totally loving. It is ultimately not a question of whether you are angry, or loving, or happy. The important thing is to be a whole person, with a full range of emotions, and to release your tensions using a meditation technique. Then you are free and can move on without carrying anything from the past.

The Master Key to Happiness

These expressive meditation techniques offer a healthy awareness of oneself. We learn to become so rooted in ourselves that we live in our center, where our inner wisdom lies. In this place we are so anchored to peace and calm that nothing can disturb us. We can then consciously choose how to respond to situations rather than react from unconscious habit. The surface of the ocean has millions of waves created by the agitating wind. But the deep-down ocean is silent, still, and calm, and no wind, no hurricane, can disturb it. We are like the ocean. If we live on the surface, agitated by every disturbance, we live in constant turmoil. But we can learn how to move down to our own silent depths where no one can disturb us.

Don't fight the hot fire of anger, don't condemn it; use it and transform it into the coolness of compassion. Using your anger and transforming it is how you become the master rather than being a victim or a bully.

When you understand how expressive meditation techniques work to transform uncomfortable emotions into productive ones, and to lead you from your agitated surface to your calm inner core, you have the master key to happiness.

Forgiving My Mother

In the introduction I talked about being terrorized by my mother as a child and how when she was ninety-four, she was finally hospitalized and diagnosed with a psychotic illness.

Walking into the hospital room, I was greeted by my mother with warmth, love, and delight. She was clearly overjoyed and grateful that my sister and I had taken the time to fly from California to England to visit her. Our visit was wonderful. My mother allowed me to help her with her lunch when it arrived, let me assist her with the special shoes she needs for her feet, and allowed my sister and me to warm up her cold hands. She showed appreciation to the nurses and kindness and gratitude to my sister. We all ended up laughing together in a way I had never imagined possible. Content and happy in her hospital situation, she expressed her thanks that my sister and I were taking care of all her affairs. Up to this point I had never experienced anything but abuse from her. For this visit I had prayed and set an intention that we would be able to have, perhaps for one last time, a kind and respectful interaction.

After many years of practicing the techniques described in this book, I was able to reach a place of forgiveness and compassion. How much of our pleasant visit was due to my compassionate, forgiving state and how much was due to my mother's medication, I will never know. I do know, however, that although my mother had been receiving medication, she was still psychotic and highly abusive. The nurses had to keep her in a private room because she shouted at the other patients on her hospital floor. Yet our interactions were full of grace.

I am grateful that, even if it was for only twenty minutes of my life, my mother and I were able to laugh and be kind to each other. The power of those twenty minutes of loving-kindness stays with me to this day.

At this point I want to introduce you to another expressive technique, the Osho Dynamic. This powerful ally helped me to express and release much of the pent-up rage, pain, and fear that had built up during my childhood and to transform these uncomfortable emotions into joy, love, and creativity.

◎　EXPRESSIVE MEDITATION: *The Osho Dynamic*

BENEFITS

The following technique is great for releasing pent-up emotions and mental stress, including anger and frustration. It shatters any preconceptions you might have that meditation necessitates sitting in silence in the lotus posture. The expressive meditations start with the body and its physical activity. Movement allows for the cathartic release of tension from the body/mind and is a powerful way to transition into sitting or lying down in stillness and silence.

The Osho Dynamic is designed for those of us who enjoy a good physical workout. It is perfect for our hyped-up lives, having little to do with the stereotypical idea of bald-headed monks sitting for hours on cold stone floors contemplating holy matters. Its message is simple: release your mental, emotional, and physical stress so that you can become physically engaged with enjoying your life *now*. It is the most vigorous technique in this part of the book and is extremely powerful in cutting through any blocks in the body/mind, bringing you to your essential self. This technique was created by Osho. A special soundtrack, *Osho Dynamic*, was created for it (see

p. 207), and I particularly recommend this one because the drumming and music urge you on past the temptation to quit. If you can't get hold of the CD, you can do just fine by setting a timer for the different stages. However, I do not recommend substituting any other music.

The words *dynamic* and *meditation* used together present us with an interesting contradiction. *Dynamic* suggests tremendous effort, while *meditation* implies silence and no effort. Yet within this very contradiction lies the possibility of bringing ourselves into balance.

This meditation has five stages. The first three — breathing, catharsis, and the Sufi mantra "Hoo!" — are designed to get us in touch with our vital energy source, our aliveness, our vibrancy. They allow for complete release and expression and should be done with vigor, so that no energy is left static in you. The idea is to exhaust your outgoing energy. When the mind has no more energy for creating thoughts, dreams, and imaginings, when it is absolutely spent, you will find that you are *in* — deeply rooted within yourself, centered, at home.

The fourth stage is silent witnessing. Coming on the heels of the first three stages, this silence is vital, alive, bubbling with life energy. It is a live silence that cannot be achieved by ordinary, rational effort. In the Zen tradition this is called effortless effort. The use of this contradictory term suggests that the process is dialectical, not linear. The energy of the earlier stages is not denied but absorbed, *used*.

The fifth stage is celebration and dance.

This meditation is best done on an empty stomach and in the early morning. I recommend wearing a blindfold to help keep your eyes closed without effort. To free up the air passages I blow my nose before starting. You'll need about sixty minutes.

STAGE ONE: BREATHING (TEN MINUTES)

If you have the CD, put it on and, standing with neck and shoulders relaxed, begin breathing rapidly through the nose, letting your breath be intense and chaotic. (If you don't have the CD, I recommend that you do this without music.) Breathe as fast as you can while keeping the breaths deep — you should feel the breath deep in your lungs. Do this as totally as you possibly can. Keep your neck and shoulders relaxed.

Keep up this chaotic breathing. (Do not let it take on a rhythm, because then you might go on automatic pilot. Keeping it chaotic helps keep you in the present moment.) You can use your arms like a kind of bellows to help pump more energy through your chest and lungs, until you literally *become* the breathing. Once your energy is moving, your body will begin to move as well. Let it happen. Use the movement to help you build up even more energy. Let your arms and body move naturally. This will help build the energy. Don't let up, and don't slow down, until the full ten minutes are up.

STAGE TWO: CATHARSIS (TEN MINUTES)

Let it all out. Just totally cut loose. Jump, laugh, scream, cry, shake, kick, punch, whatever your body feels like doing. Don't hold back. Keep your whole body moving and the sounds coming. Don't let your mind interfere; just stay in your body. Go mad.

STAGE THREE: HOO! (TEN MINUTES)

With shoulders and neck relaxed, raise both arms as high as you can without locking your elbows. With raised arms, jump up and down shouting the mantra "Hoo! Hoo! Hoo!" as deeply as possible, from the depths of your belly. Each time you land on the flats of your feet (making sure your heels touch the ground), let the sound hammer deep into your center. Give it all you've got. Exhaust yourself completely.

STAGE FOUR: SILENT WITNESSING (FIFTEEN MINUTES)

Freeze! Stop wherever you are and in whatever position you find yourself. Don't arrange the body in any way. A cough, a movement, anything, dissipates the energy flow, and the effort is lost. Be a witness to everything that is happening to you.

STAGE FIVE: DANCE (FIFTEEN MINUTES)

Spend fifteen minutes celebrating your aliveness. Dance, expressing whatever is there. Bring this energy with you into your day.

With this technique, you want to open yourself as widely as possible for the breath of life; take in as much of it as you can. Stop philosophizing, stop dreaming of the day when you'll really start living. Do it now! Live!

Whenever I do the Osho Dynamic, I am filled with exhilaration. The deep, fast breathing dissolves the cemented patterns in my psyche, making everything move and tingle, and charges my body with oxygen and life energy. Ah, yes — this is great!

If I become halfhearted about it, I shift to a higher gear. Within minutes I have reached a speed that leaves my thoughts panting behind. That is one of the purposes of the exercise: the mind is blown away. But fear not, it will come back!

All I hear now is a staccato of massive out-breaths. I realize that even more is possible (more is always possible), and I breathe more deeply yet. I am thinking nothing, there is only breathing — deeper, faster, madder. It's totally far-out. I am simply in it, and it is fun to really go for it.

When the catharsis stage starts, what a relief it is to express all my pent-up emotions, unburden my mind, and allow my body to release all its tension. Urging myself on, I discover deeply buried layers of myself, opened up by the first stage, that need expression. Long-forgotten anger, hurts, and disappointments can surface and be thrown out. All kinds of old emotional baggage can be released from my body/mind. By the third stage, I feel cleaned out and ready to fully shout the mantra "Hoo!," the sound arising loud and strong from deep within my belly. As the sound resonates through my whole body, I feel it continuing the work of the first two stages, shedding even more layers of tension. My body/mind starts to feel like hollow bamboo, preparing through this exercise to receive the silence of the fourth stage.

Suddenly I hear a voice shout "stop" (if you don't have the CD, set a timer to ring to start the fourth stage). I freeze and listen to the silence. This is the fourth stage. I sink into a profound depth of stillness. After all the noise and effort I stand stock-still, just breathing, being, enjoying, witnessing. This is it — the moment I have been waiting for. It is such a joy to discover this vibrant silence pervading my body and simply to watch.

For the dance of the fifth stage, I have plenty to celebrate. For one thing, one more Osho Dynamic is accomplished. I celebrate myself, that I have been willing to put such effort into my journey of self-discovery, releasing my tension and getting in touch with my creativity and enjoyment of life. I feel full of infinite possibilities, like an open sky.

The Osho Dynamic is a good method for anyone who feels stressed-out, neurotic, confused. It is an inner and outer workout that hews a new path through the jungle of our overly speedy minds. Many people like learning how to teach it, introducing it as an early-morning class at their local gym or at their place of work. As you well know, the more effort you put into something, the greater the payoff is. If you do this technique for at least twenty-one days in a row, you will be richly rewarded.

ACCEPTANCE

Accepting our flaws and difficult emotions and situations isn't easy, is it? We would like life always to go our way. But I have found that through acceptance of difficulties we gain deeper insight, compassion, and understanding of ourselves. There is a gift for us in every challenge, even if it takes a while to discover what it is.

The only problem with uncomfortable emotions such as anger, sadness, hopelessness, anxiety, anguish, and misery is that we want to get rid of them. When we turn the fight into acceptance, we are able to transform them. We do not want to just escape these emotions, because they are the very situations that allow us to become integrated and to grow. They are blessings in disguise.

FOUR-MINUTE MEDITATION: *Acceptance*

BENEFITS

The more your awareness and acceptance grow, the more your anger, fear, and greed simply disappear and the seed of your authentic self flowers into full bloom.

STEP ONE

This technique is very simple. First be aware of what your emotions are in this moment.

STEP TWO

Don't reject your emotions. Accept them as natural facts without any condemnation. Allow them to come to the surface. We can easily cast them off from the surface, but not so easily from the depths of our unconscious. The deeper they go, the more trouble they create, because they start functioning from unknown corners of our being. When I say acceptance I do not mean that there is no need to transform them. Acceptance *is* transformation, because through acceptance awareness becomes possible.

As you get used to this practice, you can bring awareness to the more difficult emotions such as anger, greed, fear. It is not always easy, in the heat of the moment, to remember a meditation technique, is it? To practice with anger, for example, you can, like an actor, recall an uncomfortable moment when you reacted to a situation and later regretted your reaction. You can revisit those moments in this practice with deep awareness and acceptance of yourself. Anger, greed, and fear are part of our humanity. As you grow in awareness and acceptance, you reach a point where you become aware of your reactions in the heat of the moment, and this gives you a choice: you can take a deep breath to calm yourself down and make a mental note to do the Gibberish technique (p. 65) or this technique later that evening, thus creating the possibility of *responding* to the situation, rather than reacting. If you know that fire burns you, you cannot put your hand into a flame. Awareness transforms because you cannot knowingly be angry at people, you cannot knowingly be greedy.

Embracing Our Flaws

There was once an elderly peasant in China who had two large pots, one hung at each end of a pole that he carried across his neck. One of the pots had a crack in it, while the other was perfect. At the end of the long walk from the stream to the house, the cracked pot arrived half full, while the intact pot delivered its full volume of water. For two years this went on daily, the bearer delivering only one and a half pots of water to his house. Of course, the perfect pot was proud of achieving its full potential, but the poor cracked pot was ashamed of its imperfection, miserable that it was able to accomplish only half of what it felt it had been made to do.

One day, after two years of abject failure, it spoke to the water bearer by the stream. "I am ashamed of myself, because this crack in my side causes me to leak all the way back to your house." The bearer said to the pot, "Did you notice that there are flowers on your side of the path, but not on the other pot's side? That's because I have always known about your flaw, so I planted flower seeds beside your side of the path, and every day while we walk back, you water them. For two years I have been able to pick those beautiful flowers to decorate the table. Without you, just the way you are, there would not be this beauty to grace the house."

Each of us has our own flaws. But it's our cracks and flaws that make our lives together so interesting and rewarding. We need only to take all people — including ourselves — for who they are and to look for the good in each of them.

FOUR-MINUTE MEDITATION: *Don't Ask Why* ◎

BENEFITS

As you gather confidence in the simpler activities described in steps one and two, you can move on to more complex things such as relationships, sexuality, anger, and so on. Over time you find that whatever the emotional turmoil, whatever the chattering of the mind, a part of you remains calm, relaxed, neutral. Your life flows with more grace and ease.

Asking "why" has nothing to do with awareness. Analysis is not the same as awareness. Once you ask why you feel something, you have already moved away from the simple fact of your emotion. Say you feel angry. *To be aware means not doing anything, just seeing your anger without any condemnation or evaluation, not asking about a cause*. Remain neutral. Awareness is a simple process with no questions and no answers. Simply watch.

STEP ONE

Start with very simple things, such as breathing. Do this now. Simply stay present and observe your breathing.

STEP TWO

If you get impatient, face the impatience. If you look directly at the impatience, it disappears, and you are filled with a tremendous calm. You can also do this with other simple activities such as walking to your car or doing errands downtown.

Intuitive Intelligence

Intuitive intelligence arises when we accept ourselves. When you accept, you are no longer divided. The split between you and the "should," between you and the "ought," disappears. How often have you felt, "I am this, and I should be that"? Just be yourself. How can you truly know yourself unless you go within and discover what's really there? So instead of trying to change, make the effort to know who you are and befriend that person. You have to be only yourself.

⚙ FOUR-MINUTE MEDITATION: *Befriend Yourself*

BENEFITS

As you practice this technique your self-love, self-respect, and self-acceptance become stronger. Your ability to trust your intuitive intelligence and inner wisdom is greatly enhanced.

STEP ONE

Write down one thing you like about yourself. Sit in silence, with eyes closed, and focus on this quality, accepting that there is indeed something very likeable about you.

STEP TWO

Write down one thing that you do not like, or wish was different, about yourself. Sit in silence, with eyes closed, and accept that you are not perfect, that no one is perfect. Accept yourself the way you are, including this flaw. Give yourself permission to accept who you are in this moment.

GRIEF

Have you been taught to control your feelings? Were you told that feeling grief reveals weakness? This happened to me while I was growing up. Feeling grief, however, does not mean we're weak; it means we're sensitive — and to be sensitive is to be human. Whenever we experience loss, it is natural to feel sad. It is nothing to feel guilty about. We avoid it, perhaps, because it's too much to feel the pain. We don't know what to do with all the pain.

The fact is, feeling grief and pain can be enormously healing, cleansing, and purifying. Even if it seems too much, you must allow it, for if you go deeply into your grief, you come out completely fresh and new. You come out healed, unburdened. Over time you begin to feel the grief transforming into silence, for that is what lies underneath it. Deep down we all have a calm, silent pool of wisdom and love that sustains us as part of the divine whole of the universe. If this wonderful resource has been covered over with grief, we lose sight of it. I speak from my own experience and encourage you to be courageous and patient with your own process. Embrace grief; welcome it. Allow all your feelings, even ones that may feel uncomfortable or inappropriate. For example, if a loved one has died, you might harbor some resentment, deep in your unconscious, over the person leaving you. And that's okay.

Acknowledge how much you loved the person (or pet) who is gone. Love gives freedom, in life and in death, for you and for them. Embrace this love, as you learn to embrace all your different emotions, and it will bring you deep benefits. Over time it leads you to the joy of silence.

There are four stages of grief: shock, anger, searing pain, and acceptance. The important thing is to take whatever time you need to experience each stage and to heal your grief, rather than simply burying it with whoever has died. Remember that everyone experiences grief differently. It can take a month or three years or longer to come to terms with a loss. The process can't be hurried. When we allow it, grief can take us to our deepest silence and place of wisdom.

MEDITATION: *Facing Your Grief*

Is there something you feel grief about that you have not wanted to face? It could be your lost childhood, a job, a relationship, a pet or friend who died. Sit for two to four minutes or longer and focus on it. Allow the grief to be there. Be present with it.

Sadness

Sadness is another emotion we are taught to suppress. We're told to "buck up" or to "get a grip." But these feeling are completely normal, and if we don't make room for them they become an open wound. Sadness is a very subjective experience; no one outside you can know what is best for you. The best thing to do is acknowledge it and give it its own time. Sorrow fully accepted brings its own gifts. There is alchemy in sorrow, as there is in all the difficult emotions. Sorrow can lead you to the beauty and depth of the calm, cool lake of silence we all have within, where our deepest wisdom lies.

One of the best ways I know of to heal sadness is to go for walks in nature.

MEDITATION: *Walking in Nature*

BENEFITS

> *The silence of nature has a soothing, calming effect and can*
> *help tremendously to support you in difficult times.*

In nature you simply receive the comforting silent presence of the earth, the trees, the birds, and the sky. It's important not to judge yourself but to accept your feelings and allow them to be there. Fighting them creates stress and makes things worse.

Set aside some time and go for a walk in nature with the specific focus of receiving the healing, calming vibrations from the earth, the trees, the sky, the birds, the flowers.

Here is another technique I particularly like that helps with sadness and other uncomfortable emotions.

FOUR-MINUTE MEDITATION: *Let It Be*

BENEFITS

> *When you are not depressed about your depression, and you*
> *wait, you can enter the gates of heaven on earth. Once you ex-*
> *perience this, you have learned one of the ultimate laws of life:*
> *life uses the opposite as a teacher. The opposite of depression*
> *is celebration. Celebrate everything, and trust that everything*
> *that happens is for the good.*

When you feel depressed, or any emotion that you don't like, allow it to be there. Just be aware that you are depressed. Problems arise when we judge ourselves for being depressed. Then a second depression follows. The first depression is natural and will pass in its own time. The second depression is unnatural because we are in a fight with ourselves.

When you are depressed, anxious, or worried, allow those feelings to be there with nonjudgment and compassion for yourself. Let the situation be as it is without trying to change it.

Over time, as you practice this technique, you notice your depression lifting. Be aware and alert, because when night is over, there is dawn and the sun rises once again.

The Value of Pain

It is often fear that prevents us from allowing and facing pain. The problem with this is that our minds create an extra layer of pain, inducing psychological pain. Mind is of the past and the future, never of the present. Our problems worsen when we think about our emotions rather than actually experiencing them. Reality is never the problem   our *ideas* about it are. We actually have a tremendous capacity to adjust to reality, but we cannot adjust to the future. We cannot adjust to something that is not yet a fact.

Pain exists because pleasure exists. They are complementary. Without valleys you cannot have peaks; without depth you cannot have height. If you want to avoid pain, you also have to avoid pleasure, because to have life be all pleasure and no pain is not realistic. It's like wanting two plus two to equal five, but it never will.

How do we resolve this? Accept that pain exists as a way to take you deeper into yourself, into wisdom and maturity.

MEDITATION: *The Beauty of Grief*

BENEFITS

Over time grief transforms itself into emotional stillness, love, and wisdom.

Set aside some time to be with yourself. Simply sit in silence and experience your feelings. You might want to play some sad music to help invoke them. If a person or pet has died, have with you some photos of them, or something that belonged to them — whatever reminds you of your loss, whether it's personal or global. For example, you can feel grief over the loss of more than twenty thousand lives from an earthquake in China, or you can feel it over the death of a friend.

Sitting in silence, and looking at photos or other mementos, will help your feelings to come to the surface. Do this as often as you need to.

The main instigator in my search for healing and truth was the immense pain I was in and my desire for inner peace and happiness. Once I allowed myself to really feel the pain, I was able to gain a deeper insight into life. Here I encountered the complementary nature of opposites. If there were no pain, I would not enjoy so deeply the experience of joy. For it is great pain that helps us to experience deep joy.

When we allow ourselves to experience pain, we reopen our hearts so that love, the healing force, can be received. Without pain great leaders, painters, writers, and mystics would not be able to move the world as they do. For what is pain but a doorway to deepest joy, compassion, and wisdom? If you are willing to embark on the journey, you discover the sweetness, the divine abiding that lies at the heart of pain. Comedy keeps you on the surface, whereas tragedy takes you deep into the essence of life and transforms you into a wise soul. This is a journey we make as individuals, each of us going at our own pace.

MEDITATION: *Understanding Your Pain*

Take a few minutes and see if you can gain some insight into how you avoid pain. Do you stuff food? Drink too much alcohol? Go shopping? Take too many painkillers? Watch too much TV? Fill your house or apartment with stuff? What is out of balance?

Notice, with compassion and nonjudgment, and make small, subtle changes. Practicing this every day creates space and inner fulfillment. See it not as punitive but rather as what you will get out of it. Make a pledge to yourself to bring more love and meaning into your life.

FOUR-MINUTE MEDITATION: *Healing Pain*

BENEFITS

You become so self-aware that you understand you are the host of pain, of happiness, of joy, of disappointment. These are your internal weathers — they come and go.

STEP ONE

The first step in healing pain is to accept it. Don't fight it, and don't cling to it, because fighting and clinging only make the pain worse. Allow the pain to be there, without rationalizing or judging. Simply let it be so, with tremendous compassion for yourself.

STEP TWO

Say to yourself, "I am aware of the pain," and slowly you start to disidentify from it. You create a separation, and your awareness helps you transcend your pain.

MEDITATION: *The Value of Friends*

BENEFITS

When we share, our burdens are lessened. Loneliness and despair are eased, and the flame of hope is rekindled in our hearts.

Arrange to spend time with a friend or friends, choosing only those who can be present with you in your pain. Maybe you know others who are experiencing pain or grief. Share this nonverbally, maybe listening to some soothing music, with each being with his or her own pain and yet also being present to the group. (A group meditation can be two or more people.) Or just be in silence together. Love is at its most powerful when expressed nonverbally.

Choose a calm, relaxing environment, turn phones off, and try to ensure that you will not be disturbed. The amount of time you spend on this is not important. What matters is the *quality of your presence* during the allocated time. The more present you are, the deeper will be your healing.

Experiment with the Humming meditation (p. 132) or dance your sadness. The Dancing meditation (p. 28) can also be used for dancing your sadness or any other emotions that arise.

DISAPPOINTMENT

Sometimes things really don't work out the way we'd hoped or planned. It's true, isn't it? You go to your exercise class, only to discover that every time you move, your lower back hurts. Or you realize that the relationship you thought was doing just fine really isn't working. Maybe that much-anticipated promotion doesn't materialize. How does meditation help with all these disappointments, large and small? It enables us to see where the feeling originated: from a place of hope, of expectation. You might think of hope as a good thing, and it surely can be, but it is often just a disguised refusal to be with things just as they are in the moment.

In a deep place of inner stillness we see that everything has its opposite: gain and loss, praise and blame, pleasure and pain, happiness and sadness. These are what Buddha referred to as the "terrible twins." This is the nature of our reality. In silence we can embrace these opposites. We can choose to consciously embrace pain and loss as our teachers and recognize that life itself is not disappointing; it is just a series of moments to practice being with things as they are.

I remember talking to my friend Sandra about the first time someone acknowledged her disappointment as valid. She had arranged to meet a friend one Saturday morning for breakfast and was really looking forward to it, because she hadn't seen this friend for a few years. She especially wanted to introduce her old friend to her baby. The friend didn't show up. Sandra sat there with her husband, waiting, and started to feel more and more upset. Then her husband said, "Well, that's disappointing." "Yes," Sandra replied. Nothing else was said, but Sandra remembers how powerful it was just to have it *acknowledged* that she was disappointed. She hadn't really realized how she was feeling until her husband stated it out loud. When she allowed herself to feel it and validate it, the disappointment actually transformed into a more positive feeling — feeling loved and understood by her husband — rather quickly.

How do we work with disappointment when it arises? Ideally, we start with the small disappointments and build some resources to prepare us for the larger ones.

Whenever you are disappointed (or when one of your friends, colleagues, or family members is disappointed), simply acknowledge it by saying, "I'm disappointed" or "That must be disappointing for you." Just be silent and allow the feeling to be there.

The first thing is to *consciously note the disappointment*, no matter how small. As they say in the military, when great pressure arises, you don't rise to the challenge, you fall to your level of training. If you have not practiced staying present and withstanding the emotional pull of small disappointments, you get swept away in the emotional waves of a bigger disappointment and lose perspective.

If you can stay present when something disappointing occurs, then you can *open fully to the experience*. Don't deny it, don't push it away, but realize, "Ah, this is disappointment. What does it taste like? Where is it in my body? Is the feeling expanding or contracting?" Open to the experience of disappointment, so that you can accept it and let it pass through your mind and heart. Then you can go on with your life's journey and not be frozen in place by your pain.

The next stage is to *see how in pain and confusion we cling to that which is not lasting*; that is, by contracting into our disappointment, we create our own unhappiness.

Pay attention also to lingering disappointment. Disappointment often lingers because we tend to transform our loss into a story, which keeps it alive, instead of accepting it as an event that has passed. Doing this can lock you into a ghostlike state in which you live in the past and unconsciously relinquish the freedom to move forward.

By acknowledging it, by experiencing it, you can let it go. Allow its death to be the fertilizer for what you cultivate in the life it has left you.

FOUR-MINUTE MEDITATION: *Expectation and Disappointment* ⊙

BENEFITS

Expectation keeps our mind continuously spinning. When not fulfilled it keeps us frustrated and miserable. When you drop expectation, joy flowers. Enjoy meditation, enjoy your relationships, enjoy your work. Enjoy everything intrinsically. Let the future come of its own accord. This brings you great peace, joy, and bliss.

Choose a particular situation or relationship in your life. Notice any expectations you have about how other people or the situation "should" be. Notice if you are focused on wanting things to be different from the way they are. Are your expectations out of sync with reality? The very awareness you are bringing helps you not to crash into an overwhelming disappointment if things do not work out the way you hope. Stay present, and allow things to unfold in their own way and at their own pace. You might be pleasantly surprised!

Expect nothing, be ready for everything. As you become more aware of your expectations you create a distance from your attachment to outcomes. You also find your sense of humor is more readily available.

JEALOUSY

Jealousy makes us feel disempowered and disconnected from ourselves, doesn't it? At the root of jealousy lie fear and comparison. As you uncover feelings of jealousy, try to examine what you might be afraid of. Not being loved? Losing something? Being inadequate? Being alone? Connect with the fear. Who do you keep comparing yourself to?

I remember the first time I actually told someone I was jealous. It was a powerful experience. I told a friend that I was feeling jealous because I knew another woman was interested in my boyfriend. He suggested that I tell my boyfriend I was jealous. I was so busy trying to be "cool" about it that it had never occurred to me to just *tell* him. I decided to try it. The amazing thing was that once I owned and expressed it, the jealousy I was feeling lost its charge. We laughed, and I saw how my fears were fabricating anxieties that were just causing me unnecessary stress. I also realized that by deepening my self-love, I would be less susceptible to jealousy attacks. Meditation was a vehicle for helping me to discover this.

The more deeply I acknowledged my self-worth, my value, the less fear I had that I would lose credibility if I lost my boyfriend, or, for that matter, had a less expensive car than someone else or lived in a less wealthy neighborhood. This single experience pointed me toward the fact that my value is intrinsic; it is not dependent on outer circumstances. It is up to each one of us to value ourselves, and the more we do, the more others value us.

If you are in the grip of jealousy, try the Humming (p. 132), Laughter (p. 9), and the Beauty of Grief (p. 83) meditations. These techniques are designed to increase feelings of self-love, heal the heart, and lead us to our core of silence within.

Perhaps your jealousy is not over another person but about money, possessions, other people's successes. Whatever the cause, see if you can look underneath and understand what you are afraid of. For example, if someone has a newer car than you, or a bigger house, what exactly are you jealous of? Do you think he is happier than you are because of these things? Or better than you in some way? Be careful of the trap of comparison.

Sometimes we are envious of another person's success at something because we ourselves have the potential to be successful at that same thing but have not yet manifested it. Be silent and take a closer look. Put your feelings under the microscope, like a scientist observing data, with nonjudgment. Have compassion for yourself. Look at your envy from every angle.

FOUR-MINUTE MEDITATION: *Look into Your Jealousy*

BENEFITS

As you heal the fear (and stop the comparisons!) that is underneath the jealousy, your self-love and self-esteem grow. You become stronger in yourself and regain your power. True power is knowing who you are, with compassion and acceptance of yourself.

STEP ONE

Sit with your eyes closed and choose a situation or person that triggers jealousy. Look into your jealousy, with acceptance, compassion, and nonjudgment of yourself. You will see how it's driving you crazy. Just by seeing this jealousy, you can help sanity arise — just by seeing it!

STEP TWO
Say, out loud if you can and, even better, while looking at yourself in the mirror: "I love you, _____ [insert your name here]." Make a commitment to be extra loving toward yourself every day.

FEAR

It is often fear that keeps us from meditating, from taking the journey inward to discover ourselves. Fear can paralyze us and prevent us from feeling our grief and pain. What are we so afraid of? Of being ourselves, of discovering who we are. There is, of course, a vast difference between true fear and the kaleidoscope of anxieties that choke so many people today. True fear is a survival signal that sounds in the presence of danger. It is not voluntary; it will get our attention when needed. All animals know this. Anxiety, on the other hand, is the fear that we manufacture in the mind. It is this anxiety that keeps so many of us from meditating.

In his Pulitzer Prize–winning book, *The Denial of Death*, Ernest Becker describes humans as "hyper-anxious animal[s] who constantly invent reasons for anxiety, even when there are none." Unwarranted fear has assumed a power over us that it holds over no other creature on earth. Unlike true fear, unwarranted fear is rarely logical. An awareness practice can help you tell the difference between the two.

Become Aware of Your Fears

Self-awareness can help you reverse the process of contracting in fear, and it can help you become aware of your fears. By seeing our fears for what they are and standing in them, we find that they no longer have control over us. This takes courage. I think we often mistake courage for fearlessness; it is not that at all. Courage allows us to stand in our fear without becoming controlled by it. Ask yourself what you are afraid of.

I don't mean to suggest that this is a simple question. One of my clients had the courage to admit to me that she was afraid of meditation. One would expect to be afraid of encountering a lion or a tiger in one's backyard — but encountering *ourselves?* Perhaps that is an even greater fear. I suggested that she first just allow the fear to be there.

Admitting to it out loud was a great first step. Perhaps we have learned it is cowardly or weak to say we are afraid, but fear is a natural part of life, and everyone feels it at one time or another.

Then I suggested she start with some of the simple techniques like the ones included here. Laughter and love are powerful energies for dispelling fear, and I asked her to think about how she could bring more of these into her life. It's hard to be laughing and worried at the same time! It took her some time to feel self-confident. But by accepting her fear, by allowing it to be there, she saw how it would disappear of its own accord whenever she was fully in the present moment. She saw how in the face of happiness, fear simply dissolves.

The expressive meditations that are most powerful in lessening the controlling grip of fears in the mind are the Osho Dynamic (p. 70), the Gibberish (p. 65), the Laughter (p. 9), and the Dancing (p. 28). Through practicing these techniques, you will be able to hear more clearly the wisdom of your body and heart and to act from an integrated place rather than from the controlling mind. Fear and greed live in the mind. Love, trust, courage, creativity, wisdom, compassion live in the heart. Be guided by your heart. Focus on celebration and joy.

Fear and Anger

At its root fear is connected to anger. Fear is the feminine form of anger; anger is the male form of fear. Our most natural tendency is to go into anger. We tend to go into fear when we are powerless in a situation, when there is nothing we can do. The key is to stay in whichever state comes to you, anger or fear. Sooner or later they disappear of their own accord. The dark skies clear up, and the sun reappears. By and by you become aware of what is happening. Your inner states automatically shift at some point of their own accord. Let it be so. Once you understand how this works, you become the master. You cannot start manipulating the situation, repressing the fear, or fighting it. Just allow it to be there. This very understanding is mastery. And there is no need to start trying to master it. You simply understand, and then you laugh!

How to Drop Fear

Fear is the absence of love. And the problem with something that is absent is that you cannot do anything with it directly. Fear is like darkness, which is the absence of light. There is nothing you can do with darkness directly, because it is an absence of something — which leaves us nothing to work with. But you can bring in more light.

Switch on the light. If you want darkness, switch off the light again. You work directly with the light, not with the darkness. The same is true with fear and love. Don't bother with the fear — focus on love. You can do something with love immediately. Start loving. Love is born within us; it is an intrinsic quality. We can just start giving love, sharing it, allowing it to flow out of us. As we do that, it grows. Don't hold back; don't be miserly with your love. If we don't use our natural qualities they become blocked, grow stagnant, and wither away. That's what happens to embittered people — they become frozen by their refusal to share their love. When we give love, in the very giving we become richer because our love starts radiating outward. And then our fear starts to naturally disappear. It simply cannot exist in the face of so much love. So it is not a question of dropping fear; it is a question of sharing your love, and then the fear vanishes of its own accord.

MEDITATION: *Start Loving!*

BENEFITS

The more you do this technique, over time you feel the joy in your heart expanding and your fear dissolving.

Become more and more loving, and you become more and more joyful. Don't worry about whether or not your love is returned; that is not the point. Joy follows love automatically, and fear is dissolved automatically. The beauty of love is that its result, its value, are intrinsic. Love does not depend on the response of another, because it is totally yours.

Choose a person or pet to be loving toward. It makes no difference to whom you are loving — a dog, a tree, a stranger in the grocery store. Smile at people in the street, be more loving toward yourself.

What to Do When Fear Comes

When fear comes, be with it. Be afraid. Allow it to be there, embrace it, befriend it. Feel it and understand it. Maybe it is bringing you a message.

You are like a tree standing in a howling hurricane: your leaves flutter and tremble, your branches sway, but your trunk and roots stand firm. And when the hurricane has passed, you are once again serene and peaceful like the tree, enjoying the sun glittering on your leaves, your branches at rest. Don't feel you always have to fight what comes. Fighting only creates more problems, because you are not dealing directly with the situation. You have covered up the fear with a layer of conflict, which confuses things even more. Men especially tend to do this, since in our culture, at least, they are taught not to be afraid. But fear is natural. Everyone experiences it; it is a natural part of our growth.

FOUR-MINUTE MEDITATION: *Name Your Fears* ✪

BENEFITS

Your fear's power over you diminishes, allowing you to take action and move forward.

Name your fears out loud, especially to a friend, to someone who loves you.

Or write them down. Don't judge yourself. Be compassionate, kind, and gentle. It doesn't matter why the fears are there. Don't analyze or rationalize; just look at what is. See if you can take action, despite your fears. Walk into them. If you feel afraid about doing something, ask yourself, "What am I afraid of?"

FOUR-MINUTE MEDITATION: *Moving through Fear* ✪

BENEFITS

Over time your fears calm down and disappear. You feel reassured that all is well and that all will be well. You might even discover that on the other side of fear is excitement.

If often you find yourself gripped with anxiety, try this gentle technique. Every night before you go to sleep repeat "yes, yes, yes" and get in tune with it, sway with it, let it wash over your being, from your toes to your head. Let it penetrate you. Repeat "yes, yes, yes." Let it be your prayer at night, then go to sleep.

When you wake up, the first thing to do is repeat "yes." Get into the feel of it, experience it in your very bones.

During the day, if at any time you start feeling worried, anxious, depressed, or negative, start saying "yes, yes, yes." If you can say it out loud, do so. And feel your body resonating with the words: "Yes, yes, yes."

⚙ FOUR-MINUTE MEDITATION: *Facing Fear*

BENEFITS

By facing our fears we dissolve our shadow side. The light of conscious awareness illuminates the darkness of fear and reveals the splendor of our essential being, which is pure light. We become more confident and trusting in ourselves and in life itself. We become more attuned to our inner wisdom.

Fear arises in many situations. Deep down it is always there. It is the very foundation of unconscious life. By this I mean that it is buried deep in our unconscious and fuels many of our actions. By finding the courage to stand in our fears and allow them to be there, we see them clearly and gain insight into what is at their root. We bring them from the unconscious to the conscious.

Choose a person or situation that makes you feel fearful. Look deeply into it. Continuing to stand in the fear, see what is at the root of it.

Never act out of fear. Wait until it has passed. Give it twenty-four to forty-eight hours, if necessary. Then, when you are calm and clear, take action.

DEATH AND DYING

Imagine a river with a bank on either side. It looks as if the river is creating a division between the two banks, that they are separate, disconnected. If you take the time to stand on one side of the river and look deeply into the water, you will see that the earth at the bottom of the river is of the same earth as the two banks. They are one. The division is an illusion.

Why are people so afraid of death? It's because of this illusion of separation, which is created by the mind. We think we are all separate from each other. We think that because we're in a body, we are separate from our spirit. The moment we drop the idea of separation, our fear of death disappears. When we become one with our own body and spirit and realize that we are one with this whole beautiful universe, with everything and everyone, then we know we can go beyond birth and death. This is what our search for enlightenment is about.

To get there, first you must die as an ego, because it's the ego that creates the illusion of separation. In the Zen tradition a story is told of the rope and the snake. You see a rope in the darkness of night and think it's a snake. You run from that snake in tremendous fear, trembling and sweating, and then somebody comes along, turns on the light, and says, "Oh, don't worry, it's only a rope." And that's what the mystics have been doing through the ages. They take the rope in their hand and show you that it is only a rope. All fear disappears, and you start laughing. You know, when people become enlightened, the first thing they do is burst out laughing. They laugh at themselves and at how foolish they've been. They've been running from something that never existed in the first place.

But whether or not the thing existed, the drops of sweat were real, the fear, the trembling, the sped-up heartbeat, the high blood pressure: all those things were real. And unreal things can trigger real things. A rope looking like a snake can trigger real feelings of fear and anxiety. And if you think they are real, then that's your reality. This is the whole trick of the ego. It creates a dream reality, but it can affect us. It can affect our whole life and our whole lifestyle.

When you look into this more deeply, just as you looked deeply into the river, what you're looking at is the world of the body and the world of the spirit. When we die we pass over from being in a physical body, and we return to the spirit. Our dilemma is that we are a spirit in a physical body, and for centuries we have been taught that there's a division between the two. People who wanted the spiritual life had to become monks or nuns. If you wanted to live in the world with all its physical comforts, you chose that path. It was an either-or choice. The reality is that there is no division. Just as the earth on the bed of the river connects the two banks, our inner silence and wisdom connect our spiritual and physical selves.

What are we afraid of? What are we going to leave behind? Of course, we're going to leave behind our material possessions, but ultimately when it comes down to it, most people are not worried about that. What they're going to leave behind is their loved ones. There's going to be a separation. We are going to be alone when we pass over. We're going to leave our relationships, at least on the physical plane, and this brings up so much fear that we don't want to look at it, especially if we spend a lot of time with our family and friends. *It is the desire to cling to life that creates the fear of death.*

The solution is to understand the power of love. *Love transcends death.* Love takes us beyond ego, which created the illusion of separation. We can still love someone, even though he or she has passed on. And the person still loves us. We will always be one with our loved ones; in fact, we were never separate from them in the first place. Love has the power to heal all divisions and to unite all people, creatures, and life forms in life and in death.

MEDITATION: *Love Transcends Death*

If you are close to someone who is dying, remember the power of love. It is the great healer, the great transformer, and it brings forgiveness and compassion. On your own and/or with the person who is dying, fill your heart with love. The deeper the love you have for the person, the more your compassion, for yourself and for your loved one, will overflow.

Our view of death depends on how we've been living. If we've lived each moment with mindfulness, presence, and care, then we won't be too concerned about death, because it's down the road. It's in the future, and we're firmly in the now. Even if you know someone who is close to death, remain in the now with them, cherish each moment, and trust that the love you share will keep you united.

FOUR-MINUTE MEDITATION: *Live in This Moment* ✺

BENEFITS

The more you befriend life, the more you allow yourself to love deeply, the more your fear of death disappears.

Choose a simple activity that you enjoy, such as watering your plants, playing with your cat or dog, or walking in the park. The activity doesn't matter, just the quality of your presence. Each moment look to see how you can be more alive, more in the moment, more joyful, more grateful for your life.

As you become more accustomed to doing this technique with simple, enjoyable activities, try doing it with activities you don't enjoy as much, such as doing the dishes or cleaning the kitchen floor. Then try it with the more challenging situations, for example, when a job interview doesn't go well or when someone dear to you finds out he has a life-threatening illness.

When we arrive at the moment of our death, we can be fully present and welcome it and know that it's the next step on our journey. Enlightened people just laugh. If they're drinking tea and someone tells them, "You're going to die tomorrow," they'll just keep drinking their tea. They won't be fazed at all, because they have a deep acceptance. They have no fear of death, no need to deny or reject it. People who meditate know that there is only one word to say, and that word is *yes*: yes to death, yes to life, yes to birth, yes to transformation, yes to change, yes to transition, yes to the journey. Acceptance is the key. When we can say yes to life, moment to moment, when we do come to the moment of our death, we die consciously, with great joy.

⚙ FOUR-MINUTE MEDITATION: *Know Life, Know Death*

BENEFITS
> *This technique illustrates how to bring meditation and a quality of care, presence, and love into each activity. When we transform our activities into creative acts, we transform ourselves. We experience a rebirth with everything that we do.*

Choose an activity, such as vacuuming the living room or cleaning the bathroom floor. Do it with deep care, as if the floor or the bathroom were the body of a beloved person. Suddenly, you are born anew through your creativity. *If you know life, you know death*, because deep down they are one and the same. This is what we can do. We can care about everything we do, making no distinctions between the great and the small. Let love, care, and awareness be at the very center of your life.

MEDITATION: *Being with the Dying*

If you are close to someone who is dying, be present with them. Enjoy them. Laugh, cry, and be silent with them. Understand that it is only their body that dies. Their spirit and the love you share lives on, is eternal. Fill your last times together on the physical plane with love; be grateful that you had the time with them that was granted you.

FORGIVENESS

Whatever you focus on expands. If you focus on remembering past wounds, they grow and you forget all your past joys and successes. You cannot try to forgive. You can only forgive when you understand how the ego works.

The ego exists on past misery. In moments of joy and laughter, the ego disappears, and misery disappears with it. If you live in the ego it is difficult to forgive and forget. You continue to carry with you your past hurts, humiliations, wounds, and insults. And you continue to make a story out of them.

The ego thrives on the negative, on saying no. If you try to repress it, it simply hides in your unconscious and then pops up and catches you unawares, disguised in another story. The mind can be tricky because the ego can feed off the act of forgiving. It can start thinking, "I am a great person because I have forgiven. I am better than the people I have forgiven. They are lower than me." This is where the heart comes in. If we not only forgive our enemies but love them, we move from the ego to the wisdom of the heart.

The heart does not judge; it knows only love. As we love the people who have hurt us, we grow in compassion, and the ego recedes. It has no place when love is present, when we are in the present moment, in a state of love. This is true forgiveness. And the person who benefits the most is you. Because then you are free from your past, free from your wounds, free from the people who abused you. If you go on hating them, you are still in a relationship with them. Enmity is a kind of relationship. It continues to haunt you, to invade your thoughts and spoil your joy.

The power is in our hands when we understand the workings of the ego. Focus on being in the present moment, for unless you start living in the present, you cannot forget and forgive the past. Be more alert, aware, meditative. Awareness knows only the present moment. Once the past disappears, the future automatically disappears because the future is just a projection from the past. This is your freedom. This is your power. This is the source of your well-being. Once you allow this fountain to shower you with its bounty, your life is transformed.

Understanding from the Heart

The most difficult person for me to forgive was my mother, particularly while I was still afraid of her. It took time. I focused on healing my heart, transforming my anger, and dissolving the fear that kept me trapped in inertia and the past. The techniques I share in this book helped me to transform and understand myself so that I could truly move to a place of forgiveness. I also became more grateful, because through so much pain I learned to free myself and be happy for what I had. I learned true forgiveness. Intellectual forgiveness doesn't work. It must be visceral, felt deeply in your body, heart, and soul. Give yourself time, be compassionate with yourself, knowing that sometimes you need just a bit of patience and trust to arrive at your destination.

MEDITATION: *Focus on Love*

BENEFITS

This technique helps you regain your natural state of love, joy, and peace. Your wisdom, clarity, and sense of humor return, and life is once more filled with goodness. You understand how other people cannot bring you down for long. You know how to bounce right back.

Recall a specific time when someone hurt or humiliated you. Call a friend, listen to your favorite music, talk to your cat or dog (they are great listeners), walk in nature, take a hot bath with aromatherapy oils: do whatever is nourishing for you. If you feel you need to forgive yourself, do so. Keep your focus on love, on healing your heart. Be loving, kind, and gentle with yourself. Keep the focus on you. Don't worry about the person who hurt you.

COMPASSION

Roses bloom beautifully because they are not trying to be lavender or irises. A pear seed grows into a pear tree; a hazel seed grows into a hazel tree. Practice saying to yourself, as often as you'd like, "I am happy as I am." It starts with you: when you allow yourself to be who you are, by being compassionate with yourself, you have an abundance of compassion to share. Love yourself, mother yourself, have mercy on yourself.

The problem is, most of us were not taught to love ourselves. We were taught to *get* love from others, or that we have to *do* something to become worthy of love. We were taught that we are not lovable just as we are. We learn a lot of "shoulds" and "oughts" that are impossible to fulfill. So the first step is to drop all shoulds and accept yourself the way you are.

Compassion is the highest form of love. It gives and expects nothing in return, it has no agenda. The more compassion you feel for yourself, the more you have for others. Become aware of your thoughts and actions. Observe yourself, with nonjudgment. Especially bring awareness to any self-critical or self-condemning habits you may have.

Fierce Compassion

Perhaps you were brought up, as I was, believing that compassion means being nice to everybody, however badly they treat you. I was taught not to be angry, not to raise my voice. I now know that being "nicey-nice" is not the same as being compassionate. As a result of my upbringing, I never learned to defend myself. People could verbally attack me, dump their anger on me, and I would just soak it all up. A lot of resentment and unexpressed anger got built up in me as a result. Being a "nice" girl clearly was not working. Through my years of meditation practice, I have come to understand the difference between what they call in the Buddhist tradition "idiot compassion" and "fierce compassion."

Compassion is not about having a bleeding heart full of sympathy for others. *Compassion is about having such a depth of love that you are willing to do whatever it takes to bring awareness to a situation.* Don't get me wrong. I'm not saying it's wrong to have sympathy for others. Sympathy is a wonderful quality. But the key is to bring conscious awareness to the situation. Through a meditation practice, we can slowly understand ourselves, heal our pain, release our mental, physical, and emotional tension, and bring greater consciousness to the events in our lives.

Practicing fierce compassion has taught me that by loving myself, I have more love to give to others. We can address wrongs that are done to us in a compassionate way. We can understand that mistreatment is often unconscious and that by setting clear limits, we can sometimes bring those who harm us to more awareness of their actions while, at the same time, keeping them encompassed in our hearts. We know that self-love and compassionate clarity can go a long way toward transforming even the most difficult human relationships.

Not being able to love or receive love, not being able to share oneself, causes great misery. Our soul needs love as much as the body needs food to survive. It is only through love that we know our soul and that we are more than the body/mind. It is only through love that we can feel whole. As you make a habit of remembering to love yourself, in time compassion, toward yourself and others, arises.

Live through love, live as love and miracles happen. The greatest miracle is that love gives you passion. When passion and love meet, they become compassion.

Anne's Story

Let me illustrate the contrast between idiot and fierce compassion. My student Anne works for a large insurance corporation in the sales and marketing department. She deals with people from all over the United States. Anne has a client in Wisconsin, Jennifer, whom she finds particularly difficult to deal with. Jennifer takes a long time to return phone calls and can be abrupt, sarcastic, and rude. Anne, on the other hand, is always courteous and timely with her work and strives to do a good job and to please.

As Anne became more self-aware through her meditation practice, and learned more about compassion, she began to realize why she didn't enjoy working on the account managed by Jennifer. Phone conversations left her feeling frustrated and resentful that all the work was being done on her end. Her courtesy was met with rudeness, and her hard work went unappreciated.

She decided to talk with the director of human resources and asked to be taken off this particular account. To her relief she was told she didn't have to work on this account if she didn't want to. If only she had thought to ask earlier, she could have saved herself a lot of grief.

A few months passed, and then one day Jennifer came into town on business. By chance, Anne and Jennifer found themselves arriving early for a breakfast business meeting. They started to chat, and Jennifer asked why Anne wasn't handling her account anymore. Anne took a deep breath and decided to tell Jennifer the truth. To her amazement not only was Jennifer willing to listen, but she admitted that she knew she could be a bit overbearing but had no idea she had such a devastating effect on people. She was grateful to Anne for having the courage to tell her the truth and acknowledged that she needed to make a few changes in her communication style.

She also became interested in meditation when Anne described her own work with it. Anne explained to Jennifer that she had found the Gibberish (see p. 65) and Osho Dynamic (see p. 70) techniques particularly useful in discharging her emotional stress. Anne also shared that she had then been able to sit in silence to gain deeper understanding, insight, and clarity about the situation.

Although they no longer work on the same account, Anne and Jennifer occasionally see each other and have developed a friendly relationship. By showing fierce compassion for herself, Anne was able to transform the situation, helping another person and even forging a new friendship.

Meditation techniques are a bridge to your inner world, to your wisdom, understanding, and self-awareness. Once meditation has happened, the only thing that remains to happen is compassion. Unless compassion happens, don't remain contented with meditation itself. You have gone only halfway; you have yet to go a little further. Meditation, if it is true, is bound to overflow into compassion.

In Tibetan Buddhism a great emphasis is put on developing compassion. Compassion (karuna) is said to be the "trembling of the open heart in response to suffering." Below is a commonly used practice.

MEDITATION: *Karuna*

BENEFITS

Our meditation practice unfolds most gracefully when we can experience our mind state just as it is, without any wish for the experience to be different. Compassion can become an avenue for the transformation of the difficult experience through a deep acceptance. The compassionate heart can grow big enough to hold the pain without complaining.

In compassion practice the idea is to tune into the painful aspect of a person's life. The awareness of this pain gives rise to compassion. While sitting silently, keep a sense of connection to another (or to yourself) and repeat one phrase over and over, such as, "May you be safe, may you be happy, may you be healthy, may you live with ease." You can use these or similar phrases, as long as they are positive and emphasize what is beautiful in life.

The traditional phrase is "May you be free from suffering." Another might be: "May you be free from your pain and sorrow." The phrase can reflect the particular form of pain being endured, such as, "May you be free from your grief," or fear, or illness, and so on.

Some people find that the phrase "may you be free from" can lead to a subtle sense of aversion, as though we were saying "may you be rid of." This is not necessarily what is meant in the traditional phrase, but if it strikes you that way, you might want to say instead, "I care about your grief" or "I care about your pain and sorrow."

Compassion practice is an invaluable ally in the journey of awakening. It's like finding gold on the path and can be practiced at any point in your meditation journey. It reminds us over and over that grief and pain are an inevitable aspect of life, thereby connecting us with all living beings.

The tremendous value of compassion can often be felt, paradoxically, when we are most overwhelmed by pain, whether it's our own or another's. In an incredible way the compassion practice connects us directly with the truth of our present experience.

When we utter words such as, "May I be free from pain" or "I care about this sorrow," the heart starts to soften in relation to the painful state of mind. The state seems less threatening, less alien, less overwhelming. What starts to pervade the mind, in coexistence with the difficult emotion, is the flavor of compassion, which the phrase has started to evoke. With the combination of the painful state and compassion, you experience a profound acceptance of the situation just as it is, an acceptance of yourself just as you are, and an acceptance of the human condition just as it is.

MEDITATION: *Develop Compassion for Yourself*

However you are with yourself, you are with others. If you hate yourself, you hate others. If you love and have compassion for yourself, you love and have compassion for others. Here are a few ideas for helping you cultivate compassion for yourself:

Do one thing to show compassion for yourself every day. Commit to this practice for two weeks. Then see if you can do one thing a day that shows compassion to another person.

Have a date with yourself. Take yourself to your favorite art gallery, to the beach, to a play, or to a movie. Have lunch at your favorite restaurant. Do something that is especially for you. No one else has to be considered.

Bring flowers to work to brighten your day. If anyone asks, just say they came from someone who cares about you.

Appreciate yourself. Stop and take a few deep breaths. For a few moments appreciate yourself for no reason. Appreciate yourself for the sheer enjoyment of it. Now think of one thing you really appreciate about someone you know. Let that person know in some way that you appreciate him or her.

Bring awareness to your relationships with friends, family, and co-workers. Experiencing friendship, affinity, and belonging is helpful in developing compassion. Take four minutes to sit and feel the connection with one or several people. Feel your heart opening to yourself and to them. Get in touch with the experience of having that person or people in your life.

FOUR-MINUTE MEDITATION: *Cherish Yourself, Cherish Others* ✺

BENEFITS

This technique invites you to feel the boundless love and appreciation that already exist in your heart. Your heart expands, and your capacity for giving and receiving love increases a millionfold.

We all want the same things: to be happy, loved, and loving. Sometimes we are not able to admit this to ourselves, perhaps because we believe we don't deserve it or we're afraid we'll never have it. The first step to getting something we want is to admit that we want it. By cherishing ourselves, then others, we can start to sow the seeds of love in our hearts so that they can bloom into a full flowering of love and happiness.

Breathe in, cherishing yourself, and breathe out, cherishing others. If there are people you have difficulty cherishing, cherish them anyway. You can extend this attitude to anyone you meet, from the clerk in the supermarket to the boss you don't like to your partner or parent or children; cherish the people you love (including yourself), the people you dislike, and the people you don't know.

FOUR-MINUTE MEDITATION: *Picture Yourself as a Child* ✺

BENEFITS

This technique strengthens your connection to yourself and your self-love. In turn, you will then have more love and compassion to share with others.

STEP ONE

Picture yourself as a small child, as young as you can remember. If it is difficult to visualize yourself, gaze at a picture of yourself at the youngest age possible. Send love and compassion to that small child. Maybe hug that child in your mind's eye. If it is difficult to stay with love and compassion as other thoughts and feelings intrude, gently remind yourself to come back to thoughts and feelings of love and compassion. Be careful not to judge yourself if you find this exercise difficult. Be compassionate with yourself. Just do the best you can, and recognize that it grows easier with time. (Can you see the irony of judging yourself harshly for not doing a compassionate exercise perfectly enough?)

Notice any self-hating thoughts that may creep in. You can use them as stepping-stones toward increased self-love by saying, "I've been so hard on myself, for so long, that I can scarcely do this exercise at all. I need as much love and compassion as I can allow myself."

STEP TWO

Picture yourself as an older child, and do the same thing. Don't forget to hug yourself, at least in your mind. Move up to puberty (an age when we all especially need compassion and hugs). Continue this process in steps of five or ten years until you reach your present age. Now do the same thing you've been doing for your younger selves: bathe yourself in love and compassion while hugging yourself.

If you experience any difficulty doing this exercise, just observe it. Allow it to be there, accept it without judgment. Insights and understandings about yourself will arise.

ADDITIONAL MEDITATIONS FOR TEARS

FOUR-MINUTE MEDITATION: *Confusion* ✦

BENEFITS

The heart does not get confused. It simply knows. The mind gets confused because it is trying to hold on to old rigid patterns. Recognizing what is going on helps you to drop down into your heart and trust.

Confusion is part of life. It is a good thing. It shows you are alive, growing. Accept it. The moment you accept "I don't know," all confusion evaporates. Life is a great mystery because it is based on paradox. We get confused only because we have a certain fixed idea about how life should be. The mind gets stuck on old rigidities and limitations.

Think of a situation in your life that you are confused about. Accept it. *Allow yourself to not know.* In this not-knowing there is great freedom to be in the present moment and to allow something new to arise.

FOUR-MINUTE MEDITATION: *Prayer* ✦

BENEFITS

All moments are benedictions. If you can accept with deep gratitude, nothing ever goes wrong. Try this technique for seven days. It will bring you more joy, love, and creativity.

Prayer is a silent heart full of gratitude. Trust life, trust existence, and whatever has been given to you, enjoy it. Enjoy it so deeply and with such gratitude that even ordinary things become sacred.

Choose one thing that you do not view as sacred, such as taking out the trash. Focus on this activity and see it as sacred, even if you find it difficult to see taking out trash as sacred. See it as your prayer, and over time it transforms into a sacred activity. The profane disappears when you bring it your love, grace, and gratitude. As you become accustomed to this practice, try it with more complicated situations such as with an annoying neighbor or a difficult family member.

⊗ FOUR-MINUTE MEDITATION: *Courage*

BENEFITS

> *Courage is required when it is time to stand up for our own truth and to embrace the unknown, in spite of our fears —*
> *whether it be in our relationships, in our careers, or in the ongoing journey of understanding who we are and why we are here. As we develop the inner courage that enables us to lead authentic, fulfilling lives day to day, we expand and our dreams start to come true.*

Courage is not the absence of fear. It is allowing the presence of fear, with the courage to stand in it and face what is there. As we learn where our fears originate, and understand them, we can heal them. Their mastery over us lessens, and we gradually reclaim our authentic self.

Think of a situation or person that provokes fear in you. Accept it, welcome it, and breathe. Allow the fear to be there, and see if you can understand where it is coming from. What is at the root of this fear? Notice what insights arise. Allow the fear and take action, despite it.

| FOUR-MINUTE MEDITATION: *Emotional Balance* | ✦ |

BENEFITS

Choice gives you flexibility and the capacity to practice emotional balance. This is how you remain young, creative, and lively.

When we are happy and joyful we expand. When fearful we contract, in love, in relationships, in meditation, in every way. Life is in a flow, constantly in movement. Use fear when needed — when the house is on fire, we have to escape. Fear has a natural use. But do not make contracting a habit. Develop the ability to go out, come in, expand, contract. This is flexibility. It is just like breathing. You breathe out: the chest falls down and the lungs contract. You breathe in: the lungs and chest expand. Bring awareness to your capability to expand and contract.

Notice your breathing, the rise and fall of your chest. As you become more and more familiar with your own breathing rhythm, notice if, in stressful situations or when emotions overwhelm you, you contract, continue your normal rhythm, or take big, expansive breaths. Awareness gives you a choice. The more you practice this technique when you are not in a stressful situation, the more likely you are to remember to continue your normal breathing, or take big expansive breaths, when you are suddenly overwhelmed by emotion or tension.

PART THREE

Silence

A fter the expression and release of laughter and tears, we have created a space where we can drop down into the silence that resides within us. Silence is power. It gives us vision, perspective, clarity. Creative solutions, inner peace, and wisdom all arise from silence. Stress and anxiety disappear, and we come into a relaxed balance with ourselves and our lives. Our inner silence is a constant source of love and fulfillment, giving rise to a deep sense of inner security. It provides us with an ever-present feeling of being at home, of all rightness, wherever we are, whatever we are doing. From this place we can see beyond our unconscious conditionings and beliefs and free ourselves up to become more expansive, creative, loving, and resourceful.

But bringing ourselves into balance isn't always easy, is it?

When our minds and lives are overcrowded, filled with busyness and noise, how can we function to our best potential? How can we listen to our inner wisdom, to the messages from our bodies? How do we unleash our creativity? We need silence. There are two good ways to discover silence. One is through connecting with nature. It's not that nature is absolutely silent; after all, the birds are singing, the waves are crashing on the shore. *But no more information is going into our heads.* Being closer to the earth makes it easier to stop and absorb the silence. This is why nature is so relaxing.

The other way to find silence is through the practice of meditation. *Silence is at the very core of meditation*, and all meditation techniques are designed to bring us to our core inner silence. Through the techniques presented here, you can unburden yourself from mental overload, emotional turmoil, and physical stress. As these disturbances are gradually released from your body and mind, you begin to experience the serenity of the silence that lies hidden underneath. Our power lies in facing the contradictions of our lives and in confronting and releasing the obstacles we encounter. Unburdening ourselves from turbulent emotions, releasing the noise of the mind, and understanding what causes stress in our bodies takes us to the silence of our soul, where we can embrace the happiness, satisfaction, and fulfillment that are awaiting us. We can then detach from the noise of the mind, from emotional turmoil, as well as from external sounds and chaos.

Our inner silence provides us with a place from which we can be in the world yet not be disturbed by it. Yes, we can seek out silence in distant places. We can, for instance, go to the Himalayas to meditate on a mountaintop. That would undoubtedly be an enjoyable trip. But as soon as we return to our busy urban lifestyle, our inner noise will resume, because the silence belonged to the Himalayas, not to us. The key is to find the silence within *you*. Then you can continue in your work, in your relationships with family and friends, and still have that core of silence to keep you in balance.

Silence is always present, but it is very subtle, so we must learn to recognize it. It is the life force within you, within everybody and everything. Silence is a physical experience. We hear and feel it through the belly. When we experience it we are united with all living beings. *Silence is oneness*, a state of fundamental unified existence in which all conflicts, all paradoxes, are dissolved and thus resolved.

The root cause of our stress is division. When we become sep-
arated from ourselves we feel lost. We lose our power, our wisdom, our inner anchor of peace and security. It is the mind that
creates this division. Words divide. Silence, love, laughter, and
tears unite because they are a language that everyone understands.
Silence brings us from di-vision to vision. In silence we come face-
to-face with ourselves, with the parts we like and don't like — it's
all part of the package. It's not about being perfect. It's about accepting and embracing all parts of ourselves and relaxing into
them. Silence is our true power because from this inner core come
compassion and understanding.

As you'll see, silence can also enhance the quality of our interactions and our relationships. The power of silence in our work
lives often has immediate results — in increased productivity, better decision making, and a new sense of cooperation and understanding. In love and at play, silence shows us new ways to connect
and experience joy. The down-to-earth, practical meditations in
this part of the book demonstrate how silence can benefit us even
in the most mundane aspects of our busy, overstressed lives.

Silence also brings us to that unshakable core of self-love,
where we discover that the knight in shining armor is within us
all the time. We discover that the most powerful place to be is
centered in ourselves. No one can take that away. It is our divine
abiding. And it comes unexpectedly. It's not something you can
control or demand. It has no logical sequence. It can be frustrat-
ing for the mind, which likes a logical order to things. However,
over time you accept that silence comes and goes of its own accord
and that your job is simply to create a space and to invite the silence
to show up.

As you continue to experience the gaps of silence in between
the noise it becomes like seeing into the gates of heaven — silence
— and the gates of hell — noise. The revelation is to understand

that you have a choice. And we do this not by avoiding the gates of hell — by turning on the TV or radio or grabbing the phone to call a friend — but by looking them squarely in the eye, accepting and allowing them. In this way distance can slowly be created. The techniques in this part, including the powerful expressive meditations, provide help for dealing with the gates of hell. Start to *enjoy* these gaps of silence, begin to experience them as delicious moments full of serenity and well-being, when the body is relaxed and at ease, the mind calm, the heart open and warm, and the emotions grounded and still. Your silence is without ego and its problems, without any questions or answers. It is simply silence. This is pure joy, pure love, pure light.

FROM THOUGHT TO NO-THOUGHT:
A SILENT MIND

A silent mind? I was very far away from that as I sat in seminar after seminar at an all-day Mind Body Spirit Conference in San Francisco one sunny October day, many years ago. By the beginning of the afternoon program I was tired, irritable, and on information overload. I decided that my first afternoon session, which was scheduled for an hour and a half, would be the last, and then I would call it a day. What a pleasant surprise I was in for. The presenter announced that we were going to sit in silence the entire time. I was overjoyed. We all settled down in our seats; the shuffling, rustling, and chair scraping calmed down; and we fell into a collective silence. The woman next to me, however, was having a hard time with the silence. I could hear her fidgeting with her papers and moving restlessly in her chair. After a while she got up and left, as many others did. I understood only too well what they were going through.

At first I sat with my mind spinning at breakneck speed through the information it had been deluged with since early morning. It was like sitting with an ongoing cacophony of sound as the mind sifted, sorted, and tried to deal with the information overload. When we don't give our minds time to rest we repress all the messages that are continuously pouring in. They start accumulating just like files accumulating in your in-box, like unanswered emails on your computer. And if the mind's clutter keeps on accumulating, the stress can become overwhelming.

As I sat in that room my mind rattled on with an amazing medley of thoughts about how to stuff a chicken, who to invite to dinner next week, what to wear to a party that evening, how to talk with a difficult family member, and what color the bathroom should be painted. I felt like an overstuffed chicken myself. As I continued to sit, it took a while before the noise in my mind started to subside, and I fell into a calm, cool, delicious silence, which I could feel reaching to the very depths of my being. The rest of the session was pure delight. And the extra bonus was, when I left the seminar, I felt rejuvenated and recharged, ready for the last two seminars of the day. Sitting in silence helps bring our attention to the backdrop of silence that exists behind the mind, in between the thoughts. The silence is always there. But the mind is so loud and busy that usually we cannot hear it. Between each thought and the next is a gap of silence. It is this silence that distinguishes one thought from another. By emptying the mind of its overload, by using silence practices and expressive meditation techniques, we can learn to create more space, more silence, for creative thoughts to arise, for our inner wisdom to be heard. When the silence comes, not a single thought arises. And this is the miracle — we move from heaven to hell, from thought to no-thought.

MEDITATION: *Creating a Haven*

Are you worth one minute? Sit with eyes closed. Breathe. Be present with yourself. Watch the mind with nonjudgment and compassion. Observe your thoughts as if you were watching a TV screen, creating a distance between you and the thoughts. Cherish this moment, this haven of rest in the midst of your day. Start with one minute a day, or two or three or four. Start easy. It takes time to create a habit.

EXPRESSIVE MEDITATION: *One-Minute Gibberish* ◎

BENEFITS

You gain instant relief from the chattering mind. You become more calm, relaxed, and creative.

Read the Gibberish technique (p. 65).

Do thirty seconds of Gibberish, followed by thirty seconds of sitting in silence and witnessing.

FOUR-MINUTE MEDITATION: *Watch Rush Hour Go By* ✪

BENEFITS

With a consistent practice of this technique, you start to disidentify from the mind. You are less controlled by it, more relaxed, more in touch with your inner silence and wisdom.

Sit comfortably on a chair or on a cushion. Close your eyes. Allow your body to relax.

Breathe. Now imagine yourself sitting in an armchair observing the traffic on a freeway. You see all different types of cars and trucks. Sometimes they are lined up bumper-to-bumper, and sometimes there are gaps between the cars. This is the same with the traffic of thoughts in the mind. You notice all types of thoughts, good and bad. And right now, you are simply watching all the thoughts pass by, while you relax in your armchair. You notice that sometimes the thoughts are lined up "bumper-to-bumper," and at other times there are silent gaps in between them, just as with the cars on the freeway. Watch silently, allowing the traffic of the mind to be exactly as it is. *Let the mind pass by.*

⚙ FOUR-MINUTE MEDITATION: *A Cup of Silent Tea*

BENEFITS

This practice gives you a taste of meditation, of silence, of the beauty and grace that can be brought to even the simplest of acts.

In Japan the tea ceremony is a Zen tradition that dates back thousands of years. It brings a sense of reverence and joy to the simplicity of the everyday. Do this simple practice to bring awareness to the ordinary activity of drinking tea, or your brew of choice, whether it's coffee, hot chocolate, or a cold shake.

Prepare the teacups and the teapot. Listen to the kettle and the sound it makes. Pour the tea, savoring the aroma, then taste the tea and feel that deep contentment that comes as the tea's warmth enters your body. Feel thankful that you are alive and drinking tea in this moment. Don't think about the past or future. Surrender to the present moment, as if nothing else exists, just you and the tea.

If you happen to be reading this on a sweltering day, or you live somewhere with a very hot climate, you might like to try this with iced tea. Listen to the clink of the ice as it drops into the glass; enjoy the colors through the glass, the mint, the slice of lemon, or the cherry you might add for flavor. Enjoy the coolness, the refreshing taste, the feel of the ice-cold tea as you sip it through a straw, relaxing into the moment.

If all you have time for is buying a coffee at your local coffee shop, then adapt this technique to savoring your latte or cappuccino.

RELAXATION

Meditation is based on relaxation. It is not based on control, because control creates tension. There is no fighting with the mind or with yourself, no concentration. *Just relax, watch, and let the mind pass by.* The more you can be in the present moment, not desiring anything to happen, accepting the state of affairs as is, and just being, enjoying with no expectations, the more relaxed you become. And the more relaxed you become, the deeper you can drop into your inner silence.

The Art of Relaxation

Relaxation is such an appealing idea, isn't it? But how much does it figure into your daily life? Are you relaxed as you move from one activity to the next, or is it a stressed-out rush, with never enough time to do everything?

The first step to relaxation is to remember the body. This might sound obvious, but when we are in a state of anxiety and tension we ignore our basic wisdom and common sense in favor of whatever our mind tells us is the most important thing on our never-ending to-do list. When you change the habit, starting with even just one minute a day, and create a new habit to make your body more important, a magical paradox occurs. *The more relaxed you are, the more productive you are.* Your creativity is enhanced, your health improves, and life becomes easier. Once the body is relaxed, the heart, mind, and emotions will relax in turn.

We cannot relax if our bodies are full of tension and stress. All the meditation techniques I am sharing with you begin with bringing awareness to our bodies and moving into a state of relaxed awareness. These techniques are activities that you are already familiar with, such as laughing, crying, dancing, having fun, jogging. *When we move into meditation by first releasing tension in the body, the process of coming to inner stillness goes much easier.* Begin with the body, because that is where you are. Always begin where you are — not where you think you should be. One of my favorite expressive techniques for releasing tension and coming to inner stillness is the Shaking meditation.

◎ EXPRESSIVE MEDITATION: *Shaking*

BENEFITS

The Shaking meditation is great for releasing physical stress and tension and bringing you to inner stillness and silence. If you like this technique, do it every day, or as often as you can find the time. The best time to do it is at the end of the day, when you get home from work. It's a great way to literally shake off the tensions of the day, leaving you refreshed to enjoy your evening. It can also bring you insight and clarity about your day.

This shaking meditation, which Osho created and called "Osho Kundalini," is done in four stages of fifteen minutes each, so set aside an hour for it. You can use the *Osho Kundalini* CD (see p. 207), or simply set a timer to mark the different stages. I do not recommend substituting any other music. Close your eyes for all four stages.

We begin with the body, shaking it. My students sometimes ask, "Shaking is so active, so deliberate — how can it be a meditation?" Shaking is actually a warm-up process. It's important not to force the shaking, or it will become just like physical exercise — the body will be shaking, but you will be like a rock within. Just allow it to happen, as if nobody is "doing" it.

You know how musicians spend time tuning their instruments, checking their guitar strings or the sound of the drums, preparing before they actually play the music? Shaking is like that. It is a preparation, a "getting in tune" with ourselves so that when we sit the tensions are dissolved and the space of meditation descends on us.

As the shaking takes over it begins to penetrate to the very core of your being. Your whole body becomes a turmoil of energy, a cyclone. This is continued in the second stage. Through the energy of the cyclone you can then reach the center. This is a preparation for the third and fourth stages, when you will be silent and still, open to receive the guest of meditation.

STAGE ONE: SHAKE IT (FIFTEEN MINUTES)
Standing comfortably, with eyes closed, just let your whole body shake, feeling the energies moving up from your feet. Let go. Feel yourself become the shaking.

STAGE TWO: DANCE (FIFTEEN MINUTES)
Let your body move in any way it wishes. Dance.

STAGE THREE: BECOMING STILL (FIFTEEN MINUTES)
Now, either sitting or standing, be still. Relax deeply within yourself. Be aware of your breathing and witness any thoughts or emotions, with no judgment. Don't cling or reject; simply accept what is. Allow the silence of meditation to descend on you.

STAGE FOUR: LIE DOWN AND BE STILL (FIFTEEN MINUTES)
Now, without opening your eyes, lie down. Just lie there in stillness for another fifteen minutes.

When I do this meditation I find it helpful, in the first stage, to imagine myself as a rag doll shaking out all the tensions from the body/mind, remembering in particular to shake my head a lot if I have had a very mentally stressful day. I like to keep my feet firmly planted on the ground so that I stay rooted in myself and don't tip over. I find that this allows me to experience greater flexibility of movement in the shaking. It's a good idea to keep your knees slightly bent, remembering to shake the legs, hips, upper torso, shoulders, arms, hands, and head. This is an extraordinarily gentle yet powerful way to release stress and free up the body from any straitjacket it has been in, such as sitting in the car or in front of the computer.

The sense of freedom carries over into the second stage. You can use the dance to release and express any kind of emotional stress, such as frustration, anger, sadness, and disappointment and also to express any playfulness, contentedness, and joy you might be in touch with that day. It is surprisingly refreshing to get in touch with ourselves nonverbally and to allow the more hidden or repressed parts to come out into the open. This is a great way to get to know ourselves and to gain clarity and insight into whatever is going on in our lives at the moment.

After all the physical expression and release, to then sit or stand is both relaxing and an opportunity to witness whatever is happening with ourselves, compassionately and without judgment.

Finally, when we lie down in silence, the body, fully supported by the floor, can sink into a deep relaxation. This depth of relaxation allows the energy generated by the first two stages to take our meditation to the deepest corners of our being.

Create a Rhythm

Rhythm has a calming effect on the body/mind. Over the years I have noticed that I have come to talk more slowly and carefully.

Remembering to breathe with awareness before I speak helps, especially in a crisis. It reminds me to come down from the head and into the body. Staying connected with the body helps me stay connected to myself. The Humming (p. 132), Shaking (p. 128), and Dancing (p. 28) meditations help us tune our bodies into their natural rhythm.

Meditation is about *paying attention*. It's that simple. When we are small and learning to walk, we are totally present with each step, totally conscious that right now we are putting the right foot in front of the left. We are in our bodies. As we get the hang of it and the body acquires the knack of walking, we go on automatic. We are not present anymore with the walking; the body knows how to do it and we are somewhere else; we become disconnected from our bodily movements.

Begin with the Body

To be beneficial, meditation must be grounded in the body. There is a Hasidic tale about a great rabbi who was coming to visit a small town in Russia. It was a very great event for the Jews in the town, and each thought long and hard about what questions they would ask the wise man.

When the rabbi finally arrived, all were gathered in the largest available room, and each was deeply concerned with their questions. When the rabbi entered the room, he felt great tension. For a time he said nothing, and then he began softly humming a Hasidic tune. Presently everyone hummed along with him. He then began to sing a song, and soon all sang along. Then he began to dance, and soon all present were caught up in the dance too. After a time all were deeply involved in the dance, all fully committed to it, just dancing and nothing else. In this way, everyone there became whole with themselves, healing the splits within that kept them from understanding. After a time, the rabbi slowed the dancing to a stop, looked at the group, and said, "I trust I have answered all your questions."

When we become completely absorbed in bodily movement, we are brought slowly and gradually to doing just one thing at a time. As we move out of our heads and into our bodies, all our questions disappear, with only the sheer enjoyment of the activity remaining. An effective way to relax the mind and begin meditating is with a bodily activity. If the body does not feel the benefit, then your heart, mind, and soul will not either. The techniques in this part of the book are designed to help you come to an effortless moment. Just being. Doing nothing. Relaxing into the present moment.

◎ EXPRESSIVE MEDITATION: *Humming*

BENEFITS

Humming is a technique designed to open us to trust, to bring us into our inner sanctuary of peace and serenity. It has ancient roots in Tibetan Buddhist techniques. As we hum we generate our own energy to heal and center ourselves. Humming brings us straight down from the head and into the body, keeping us alert yet relaxed. The sounds resonating throughout the body/mind have a soothing, calming effect. It is particularly good for healing the heart on both the emotional and physical levels, for releasing emotional distress, and for bringing us to a balanced state of deeply centered well-being. It is also helpful for anyone who suffers from throat, bronchial, lung, or chest problems or who has communication difficulties, and it is ideal for singers or speakers or anyone who wants to become a singer or speaker.

Mitchell L. Gaynor, MD, one of New York's most prominent oncologists and director of Medical Oncology and Integrative Medicine at the Strang-Cornell Cancer Prevention Center, has used the incredibly healing power of sound in his clinic and shown how it can dramatically improve health, reduce pain and stress, and awaken creativity. He has had patients go into remission after using healing sounds.

In his book *The Sounds of Healing*, Gaynor cites Dr. David Simon, medical director of Neurological Services at Sharp Cabrillo Hospital in San Diego California, and medical director of the Chopra Center for Well-Being, who has seen that healing chants and music have "measurable physiologic effects." Simon points out that chants are actually metabolized into natural painkillers, releasing healing agents into the body.

The humming technique I like to use is called Osho Nadabrahma. Nadabrahma is an old Tibetan technique, updated by Osho.

I recommend this expressive technique for anyone whose health makes her not suitable for the more energetic and cathartic methods. It is also great for recharging your batteries when you're running on empty.

You can do Osho Nadabrahma at any time of day, either alone or with others. You will need about an hour and a quarter for it: approximately an hour for the meditation and, very important, fifteen minutes afterward for remaining at rest.

The *Osho Nadabrahma* CD was created to complement this meditation (see p. 207). If you choose not to order the CD, the meditation can certainly be done without it. However, I do not recommend using any other music for this technique

STAGE ONE: HUMMING (THIRTY MINUTES)
Sit in a relaxed position with eyes closed and lips apart. Start humming until you can feel the vibration throughout your body. (You'll probably be humming loudly enough to be heard by others.)

Just breathe comfortably; no special breathing techniques are needed. You can also alter the pitch of your voice or move your body smoothly and slowly, if you feel like it. A point will come when the humming seems to continue by itself and you become the listener. Continue humming for thirty minutes.

STAGE TWO: CIRCLING WITH THE HANDS (FIFTEEN MINUTES)
If you're not using the *Osho Nadabrahma* CD, set a timer for seven and a half minutes. I recommend using a timer with a pleasing bell. You don't want to be jarred out of your meditative state.

Now, still sitting and humming with eyes closed, place your palms up and, starting at the navel, move both hands forward and then separate them to make two large circles mirroring each other, left and right. The idea is to move your hands in an outward circular motion. You bring the hands back toward the navel with the palms up and continue making slow circles, parallel to the floor. The movement should be so slow that at times there will appear to be no movement at all. Feel yourself giving energy to the universe.

After seven and a half minutes turn the hands palms down and start moving them in the opposite direction. Now the hands will come together toward the navel and then circle outward away from the sides of the body. Feel that you are taking energy in. As in the first stage, if you feel like moving any part of the rest of your body, do so slowly and mindfully.

STAGE THREE: REST (FIFTEEN MINUTES)
Now sit or lie absolutely still for fifteen minutes. (And take it easy for at least fifteen minutes after doing this technique.) Get up slowly, being mindful of not rushing into your next activity. You will feel a profound sense of well-being, of balance between your inner and outer worlds. Enjoy it. This powerful humming technique opens up a whole new world of healing, comfort, and creativity to you.

Don't Force It

Relaxation cannot be forced. It is a "nondoing," an allowing, a being. It is a state of letting go. When you try to relax, a subtle tension is created. Shift the emphasis from "trying" to "letting go." Let me illustrate. Imagine you are holding a tennis ball in your hand. Now try dropping it. Of course you cannot *try*, because all you have to do is open your hand and let go. The same is true of relaxing into meditation. You just open yourself up, let go, and drop down inside yourself.

The techniques that follow assist you in opening up and letting go of your frustrations, tension, and restlessness.

Leave Effort Behind

In the Zen tradition, the masters say to the disciples, "Just sit. Don't do anything." Like the disciples, at first many of us try to just sit. But by and by, when you remember to go beyond trying, a moment comes when you are not doing anything about relaxation; you are just being there, aware, and it happens. Again, this inner transformation cannot happen through effort because effort creates tension. But by making effort at the beginning, you also become capable of leaving effort behind. This happens of its own accord — it is not something you can control. This is the effortless effort I have been referring to.

As you make a practice of relaxing and focusing on awareness of your body you gain understanding of how you keep yourself busy or of how obsessive you are about staying in some activity. The more relaxed you are, the more you allow insights and understandings to arise. You might like to try my *Guided Relaxation and Meditation* CD (see p. 206). This awakening to who you are is the heart of meditation.

⚙ **FOUR-MINUTE MEDITATION:** *Breathe*

BENEFITS

> *This is one of the quickest ways to dissolve tension and relax the mind and body. You might also like to try my CD* Wisdom of the Body *(see p. 206).*

One of the simplest and most effective practices for bringing us fully into the present is conscious breathing — just remembering to come back to the breath, to breathe in and out, in and out, steadily.

When we are tense or anxious our breathing becomes shallow; sometimes we even stop breathing for short periods without realizing it. The simple act of conscious breathing brings us out of our heads and into our bodies, into the present. Breathing in, breathing out. Yes, it's that simple. Do it right now.

⚙ **FOUR-MINUTE MEDITATION:** *Slow Down Every Process*

BENEFITS

> *When you practice this technique consistently, more inner wisdom is present in your daily activities. Your health, relationships, and productivity are greatly enhanced.*

Focus on slowing down some of your daily activities. For example: walk in a relaxed way, eat in a relaxed way, talk and listen in a relaxed way. Even if you are in a rush, rush in a relaxed way, with the awareness that "right now I am rushing."

⚙ **FOUR-MINUTE MEDITATION:** *Sit and Do Nothing*

BENEFITS

> *Over time, your busyness, your obsession with activity, falls away. You become at ease with yourself. Inner peace and serenity effortlessly arise in you.*

Sit and do nothing, with no agenda, simply being. *Relaxation means no information is being thrown into you.*

| FOUR-MINUTE MEDITATION: *Smile Gently When You Breathe* ✺ |

BENEFITS

Smiling relaxes the muscles in the face and body. It encourages your natural inner joy to come to the surface. You feel more positive, alive, and relaxed.

Smile gently when you breathe. Do it right now.

NONJUDGMENT

Judgments can fill the mind with such incessant chatter that it's hard to think clearly, isn't it? They burden us with memories from the past and projections of the future. It's like looking at life though a dirty window. How can we wipe the window clean and see clearly? How can we find the silence that waits patiently for us underneath all the noise and brings us peace, calm, and clarity? Practice nonjudgment. As you make a habit of this and allow all judgments, good and bad, to pass by on the screen of the mind, you discover that silence is right there for you, just like the sky is always there, even when hidden by clouds. And in that silence you find the real you.

Trust Yourself

Karen wanted to be a singer for as long as she could remember. As a child she liked to sing and hum to herself as she played. She had four older brothers who laughed at her when she sang because they were interested only in rough-and-tumble games and called her a sissy. Over the years, Karen stopped singing.

When she came to see me, she was working in an insurance office dealing with claims. She wasn't happy with her life. As Karen learned meditation and practiced watching the judgments of the mind, she became aware that she was repressing her joy and passion for singing because of painful memories of her brothers' remarks. The effect of their judgments had caused her to shut down her joy of singing for fear of being laughed at. This had also led her to judge herself.

Karen had difficulty accepting herself the way she was and accepting one of her passions in life. Why is this the case for so many of us? Why is it so difficult for us to accept ourselves the way we are? There are two reasons. First, we often learn plenty about what is wrong with us, as Karen did, but very little about what is right with us. So we grow up feeling insecure, inadequate, and fearful, wondering if we will ever be okay. Through meditation, we can put a halt to this stream of criticism and judgment and reclaim ourselves. By observing judgments passing across the mind we can learn to adopt an attitude of nonjudgment toward ourselves.

But there is still another part to this answer. We are all born with a potential to fulfill, whether it is to be an interior designer, a stay-at-home parent, a cook, a software engineer, an artist, or a hair stylist. And until we are on our path, heading in the direction of fulfilling our creative potential, we will be dissatisfied with ourselves.

As Karen rediscovered her passion for singing, she found a far greater acceptance and contentment with herself and her life.

Deep down our soul is discontented until we start moving in the direction of what gives passion and meaning to our life. Once again, meditation can be a powerful part of this self-discovery process.

It is the nature of the mind to judge and compare, and we don't have to feel bad about this. It just is. So watch out for judging yourself for judging! Simply notice, become aware, like a scientist observing data. Accept the judgments, and let them pass by. Don't fight with them, try to hide them, or push them down into the unconscious. By doing so we create trouble for ourselves. Bring them out into the open, see them, admit to them, accept them. They then pass by without clouding our vision. Practicing nonjudgment is like cleaning your glasses so you can see more clearly and your inner silence is more readily available.

MEDITATION: *Nonjudgment*

If you find yourself making negative judgments about a person in your life, for example your boss, a co-worker, an employee, your mother-in-law, or your spouse, take some quiet time and ask yourself these questions:

- Am I thinking in ways that tend to be overly negative?
- Are my expectations realistic?
- Would an objective observer view or interpret this situation differently?
- Will this make any difference to me in a week, a month, a year, or ten years?

Notice when judging what happens in your body, the sensations and feelings. Do you notice a contraction, a shrinking?

When you find you are making negative judgments about a person, make a practice of sending them a blessing, of wishing them well. See if you can incorporate that person into your heart, despite what you don't like about them, and see how much better that makes *you* feel.

FOUR-MINUTE MEDITATION: *Walking down the Street*

BENEFITS

This shift of perspective brings you more in touch with yourself, helps you become more deeply rooted in yourself. Your self-confidence and self-trust are greatly enhanced. When you remove judgment, love appears.

Next time you're walking down a street, or sitting on a park bench or in a coffee shop, notice how you judge people as they pass by;

for example, the way they dress, whether they smoke, are over-weight, are chewing gum, how loudly they talk, what kind of car they drive. Bring your attention inward, to observing your mind and the judgments it is making about what it sees. The knack of it is to bring your attention from the people, outside you, to yourself, and what is going on inside you. For example, as you walk down the street, first bring your attention to yourself, to your feet on the ground, to your breathing, to the swing of your arms. Become aware that "in this moment I am walking down the street." And now, observing the passersby, notice any judgments passing across your mind.

Whenever you are walking down a street, do this, even if it is just for a moment or two. Have fun with it!

FOUR-MINUTE MEDITATION: *Looking without Judging* ⚫

BENEFITS

By opening your vision, your heart, and your mind in this way, you will find a greater flexibility, openness, and receptivity within yourself to the world at large.

Look at a flower or some other small thing for a few minutes. Don't say "beautiful" or "ugly." Don't say anything. Don't bring in words. Simply look. The mind will feel uncomfortable; it would like you to say something. Try to ride through this feeling and just look.

Start with neutral things, things that don't hold any charge for you: a rock, a flower, a tree, the sun rising, a bird in flight, a cloud moving in the sky. Only when you have gotten used to the technique should you try it with people. As you begin to look at people without judgment, you will see them more clearly and with more compassion.

WITNESSING

A man came to the Japanese Zen master Ikkyo and asked him for some words of wisdom to guide him in life. Ikkyo nodded agreeably and wrote on a piece of paper the word *attention*. The man said he did not understand and asked for something more. Ikkyo wrote, "Attention, attention." After a further request for an explanation, Ikkyo wrote his final statement for the man: "Attention, attention; attention means attention."

The special knack of meditation is to develop the one who pays attention, the witness. Known also as watching or awareness, witnessing is a mirrorlike quality of being present to what is, without judgment. It is a capacity we all have. When we do a simple sitting meditation, we sit comfortably with our eyes closed and just begin to watch the energies that move within us all the time: thoughts, physical sensations, emotions. We develop the knack of simply watching these distractions go by with acceptance. You can be a witness to the events happening inside you and also all around you. It becomes possible to be aware of both your outer and inner realities at the same time.

The essential core of meditation is learning how to witness. How do we acquire this knack? We begin by being a witness to the mind, by becoming separate from the mind. Here let me say that the problem is not the mind per se. The problem is your *identification* with it. You think you are the mind. Disidentify from it. Be the watcher and let the mind be there — watched, witnessed, observed. When you watch a dog, you are clearly not the dog; when you look at a tree, you are separate from the tree. The same applies to the mind. Watching is the key. Watch the mind, without repressing, without preventing, without judging, and slowly you begin to disidentify, realizing that you are not your thoughts, your physical sensations, your emotions.

I like to use the image of a frog on a lily pad. When a frog is on a lily pad, resting but ready to move, it is alert and awake, yet its body is relaxed. The frog is totally present, observing the activity of the pond, waiting for the right moment to jump. It is not in the grip of fearful thoughts, which might take it into the past or the future, nor is it contracted by anxiety, which might impede its ability to jump. It is free.

Just learn to transcend the mind through the witnessing technique. This brings respect for the mind, which can then function far more efficiently. When you become the watcher, your mind can have some rest, now that it is no longer carrying unnecessary weight. Otherwise, if your mind is constantly working, you experience a deep mental fatigue. Allow the mind to become an instrument in the hands of you, its master. Patience is needed, but this witnessing technique brings rich rewards. It is a thread of awareness we can weave into the fabric of everyday life.

Do this: move your right hand without any watchfulness. Now move it again, this time watching from *inside* the whole movement. Do you see how different the two movements are? They are qualitatively different. The first action is mechanical, robotic. The second is conscious. When you are conscious you feel the hand from within. You are more aware.

Befriend the Mind

It is not that meditation is against the mind; rather, it is *beyond* the mind. The mind is our bridge from the subconscious to the conscious, our gateway of expression to the outer world. Be grateful for it. Find ways to appreciate the insights, understandings, and creativity it brings. See it not as an enemy but as a friend.

As this friendship with the mind deepens, your mind no longer disturbs you during meditation. You are not fighting it; you are simply letting its thoughts pass by. This is the soil in which the roses of meditation can blossom. When we befriend the mind, allowing it to subside into its natural place in the background, our qualities of relaxation, humor, compassion, awareness, and self-acceptance flower.

Whatever you are doing — walking, sitting, eating — do it watchfully. Or if you are not doing anything, just breathing, resting, relaxing in the grass, become aware that you are a watcher. Yes, you forget, over and over again. You get involved in some thought, some emotion, some sentiment — anything to distract you from being the watcher. Just remember with compassionate nonjudgment, and return to your center of witnessing.

When you make this a continuous inner journey, you are surprised at how radically life can change. Once we reach that place of being the watcher, the witness, we see ourselves with more clarity and objectivity. We see the dramas in our lives with perspective and compassion, and insights and understandings arise naturally.

The mind and the ego want to make it complicated, but it is not. Mind always wants to control. But watchfulness goes beyond the mind's control. It is beyond it, above it; it is like a death to the control our minds have over us.

Listening to Music

Listening to music can help us understand this process of watching and becoming aware of the gaps between our thoughts. Between one musical note and the next is a gap of silence. It is this silence that distinguishes one note from another. Likewise, there is silence between each of our thoughts. When we pay attention, we start to notice this background of silence that is always there.

MEDITATION: *Listen to Music*

BENEFITS

The liberation you feel once you realize that you are not the mind can be extraordinary. There is no more anxiety. You are at ease, in a deep let-go. You know you can drop down beyond the mind to your inner haven of peace and stillness

Listen to some music that is not overcrowded with notes. I particularly like *Zenotes* by Shastro and Nadama (see p. 207), and also the music of Manish Viyas (see p. 207). Sit down and close your eyes. As you listen to the music, notice the notes and bring your awareness to the gaps between them. You will find this deeply relaxing as it invites you to be more aware of your own inner silence. You can also try my CD *Witnessing the Mind* (see p. 206).

Be Aware of What You Put into Your Mind

Think about what you put into your mind. When you watch scary movies and/or listen to anxious people, for example, these thoughts transmit into your mind and create all kinds of trouble for you. They feed your fear. You can choose to be more discerning and feed your mind positive, uplifting thoughts.

I don't mean be an ostrich with your head in the sand, disconnected from reality. Keep a balance, remembering to feed your mind with beauty. Then when you are watching the mind in meditation, at least you are watching more positive thoughts.

Think about decorating your mind the way you would your body. You keep your body clean, you keep it fresh with sweet-smelling fragrances because you want your body to be loved and respected by others. In a similar way, decorate your mind with great art, poetry, music, literature. Then your mind has a music and a poetry all its own. And it is easier to transcend.

MEDITATION: *Vipassana*

BENEFITS

Vipassana practice allows us to see the true nature of reality as a constantly changing process, and we begin to accept all aspects of life — pleasure and pain, fear and joy — with increasing equanimity. Grounded in the present moment, our awareness leads us to a deep stillness that can give us a growing understanding of the nature of life. From this insight, wisdom and compassion become truly possible.

Vipassana is a traditional one-hour Buddhist meditation developed 2,500 years ago. If one hour is too much for you, start with four minutes: two minutes of sitting and two minutes of Zen walking.

STEP ONE: SITTING (FORTY MINUTES)

Find a place to sit. It doesn't have to be a silent place. Experiment until you find a place you feel relaxed in. A chair might help, or a meditation bench or an arrangement of cushions. Sit with your back and head straight but not rigid, with eyes closed and the body as still as possible. If you need to move a part of the body during the sitting, do so slowly and with awareness, saying to yourself: "Right now I am moving my arm" or "Right now I am stretching out my legs." (Remember that meditation is not about getting it "right" or "wrong"; it is not about torture but about *awareness of whatever is happening*.) Over time, as you practice, the mind quiets down and ego disappears. You are still there but with no feeling of "I." You have opened the doors and now you wait, with your loving, trusting heart, for the moment of silence, joy, and serenity to arise.

Remember not to be too serious. Nothing special is supposed to happen. There is nothing to figure out or analyze, no success or failure. You are simply allowing yourself to be less identified with the body, mind, emotions, and environment, which then leaves space for insight or understanding to arise.

Let the mind pass by. These are the five key words for watching the mind. There is no concentration, for concentration creates tension. There is no forcing, no trying to stop the mind, no fighting with the mind. Just let the traffic of the mind pass by. You are the watcher, observing, disidentified, with no judgment, accepting whatever passes by. It is as if you were sitting high up on a mountaintop, watching life pass by with no attachment or involvement. This practice brings you to your essential self.

Vipassana can be done three ways. Try them all, or choose the one that suits you best.

Awareness of actions. There are three classic ways of suffering; by clinging, by rejecting, or by wanting clarity when the mind is confused. This practice teaches us acceptance.

As you sit silently, if your leg begins to ache, move it to a more comfortable position with awareness, knowing consciously that you are moving your leg in that moment. Whatever thoughts are passing across the screen of the mind, just be a watcher. Don't cling or reject. Whatever emotions pass by on the screen of your heart, just remain a witness. Don't get involved, don't get identified, don't evaluate what is good, what is bad. Simply dwell in *a state of alertly wakeful attention that clings to no content and is not directed toward any object.*

The idea here is to reach a choiceless awareness. Be like a scientist observing data, with no judgment. Instead of thinking, "I am sad," say to yourself, "There is sadness around me; there is joy around me." Just watch the emotion or mood. You are a watcher on the hills, and everything else is going on in the valley. Watch whatever comes up as clouds passing in the sky, neither clinging nor rejecting.

Awareness of breathing. The second practice involves becoming aware of your breathing. There is no special breathing technique; ordinary, natural breathing is fine. As you inhale, your belly naturally rises up, and as you exhale, your belly settles down again. Become aware of the belly, its rising and falling. It is really your life energy, the spring of life, that is rising up and falling down with each breath.

As you become more aware of the belly, the mind naturally quiets, the heart becomes silent, and moods disappear. While the first technique involves becoming aware first of your body and then of your mind, your emotions, and your moods, this technique is much simpler: just feel the belly moving up and down. Women often prefer this one.

Awareness of breath through the nostrils. The third technique involves awareness of the breath passing through the nostrils. Unlike the belly breathing technique, which brings warmth, this technique brings a certain coolness. Men often prefer this technique. Just feel the breath coming in through the nostrils and going out, coming in, going out . . .

Once you've tried all three techniques, you may find that you prefer one or that you like to do two together. Or you might even like a combination of the three. Do whatever feels easy. Remember, easy is right.

STAGE TWO: ZEN WALKING (TWENTY MINUTES)
If you are doing a shorter version — four minutes, for example — follow two minutes of stage one, sitting, with two minutes of "Zen walking." This stage involves slow, ordinary walking based

on the awareness of your feet touching the ground. While you walk, your focus should be on the contact each foot makes with the ground (or floor). Keep your eyes lowered so that you can see only the ground a few steps ahead. Be alert to the movements of your body.

OPENING THE HEART: SILENCE IN LOVE

Have you ever found yourself going from one relationship to the next? Or have you experienced the push-pull, wanting to be alone yet also in the relationship? Are you afraid of being lonely? Of commitment? I want to share some secrets I have discovered about love and how being in touch with our inner silence brings deeper insight and understanding to some of these dilemmas that perplex us.

Love is a state of being. It is not about anybody else. It starts with you. If you don't love yourself, you will never be able to love anybody else. The more you love yourself, and draw on the infinite source of love from within your own heart, the more your heart expands and you begin to experience love and joy *for no reason*. Falling in love with another person helps us with this process. First of all, love is a great energy pull. It is not that you do something; it's that you are pulled in, aren't you? Love has such a powerful magnetic force. You gravitate toward the object of your love, almost helplessly, sometimes even against your will — that's why we call it "falling in love." Who can avoid it?

Second, whenever you fall in love, suddenly you are no longer ordinary; something miraculously changes. *Love transforms you.* Love is miraculous — it transforms base metals into gold. Have you watched people's faces and eyes when they fall in love? Have you experienced this? You can hardly believe that they, or you, are the same person. Love transforms earth into sky, the human into the divine.

So love is an energy field, and it is a transforming force. It helps you to become weightless — it gives you wings. It is through love that you move into the divine, for *love is divine energy*. Whether or not you are religious makes no difference: love remains the central experience of human life. It happens to everyone, more or less, and whenever it happens *it transmutes you. It is the bridge between you and the divine*, between you and enlightenment.

Love and Meditation

Love and meditation are inextricably intertwined. The path of love leads to meditation, and the path of meditation leads to love. When two people fall in love, they drop their egos, hypocrisies, and masks — they want to be together, almost as one soul with two bodies. That's the desire of love. This is a beautiful opportunity to transform this energy into a meditation and to bring the balance of love and meditation into your life.

FOUR-MINUTE MEDITATION: *Opening to Self-Love* ❂

BENEFITS

> *This technique allows you to open to your own intrinsic and unique beauty and to rediscover your essential value. It brings you deeper insight, understanding, and self-healing and opens the way for more positive and loving relationships with others.*

If you totally accepted yourself just as you are, would you have any problems at all? Sit silently and see if you can gain insight into the ways you reject yourself. What fears and beliefs stop you from being loving and compassionate with yourself? When you gain a clearer understanding of these inner mechanisms, the old habits of self-rejection and doubt begin to fade away.

What you can learn from the failure of love is to become more aware, more meditative. And by meditative I mean capable of being joyous while alone, of releasing your imprisoned splendor. And you become so joyous, such a celebration arises within you, that all need of relationship disappears. And yet you can still relate with people. You can still be in an intimate relationship. You have understood the difference between aloneness and loneliness. You have found the benediction of your essential self.

Love is a natural kind of meditation. And meditation is a divine kind of love. *Love starts with oneself.* It's about befriending who we already are. The critical mind constantly tries to judge us, to tell us that we should have done this or we ought to have been that. Our effort must be to embrace ourselves in our own hearts, to have compassion for ourselves, to love ourselves every day, no matter what. And I don't mean trying to be "perfect" in the usual sense. My definition of perfection is being true to yourself at any given moment.

Perhaps you have learned to be false to yourself in order to please other people and to be who they want you to be. Love means accepting your true self. It means living each moment from your truth, expressing yourself without fear, allowing your emotions, thoughts, and physical sensations to be what they are without judgment. Then being in relationship with others can help you ripen and mature, can lead you deeper into yourself. To love and accept yourself is meditation. To love another is love, the other side of the coin. In loving yourself the energy goes within; in loving another, the energy goes without. We need both, and to understand and experience the dance between love and meditation is the greatest benediction life has to offer.

Choiceless Awareness

A story is told about the twentieth-century Russian mystic Gurdjieff, that when he was nine his father was dying and called him close to his bed. He whispered in his ear: "My son, I am not leaving much to you, not in worldly things, but I have one thing to tell you that was told to me by my father on his deathbed. It has helped me tremendously; it has been my treasure. You are not grown up yet, you may not understand what I am saying, but keep it, remember it. One day you will be grown up and then you may understand. This is a key: it unlocks the doors of great treasures."

Then his father said a very simple thing: "Whenever somebody insults you, my son, tell him you will be silent and meditate over it for twenty-four hours, and then you will come and answer him."

Gurdjieff could not understand what was so valuable about this advice. But because it was given to him by his dying father, who had loved him tremendously, it became imprinted on him. He could not forget it. Whenever he remembered his father, he remembered the saying. Without truly understanding it, he started practicing it. If someone insulted him, he would say, "Sir, for twenty-four hours I have to go and be silent with myself and meditate over it — that's what my father told me. And I cannot disobey my father. He loved me, and I loved him. You can disobey your father when he is alive, but when he is dead, there is no way to disobey him. So I will come back after twenty-four hours and answer you."

Gurdjieff has said that this practice changed his life, giving him the greatest insights into his being. Sometimes he found the insult to be accurate. So he would return to the person and say, "Sir, thank you, you were right. It was not an insult, it was simply a statement of fact. You called me stupid; I am."

Or sometimes it happened that after meditating for twenty-four hours Gurdjieff would come to know the insult as an absolute lie. But when something is a lie, why be offended by it? So he would not even bother telling the person that it was a lie. A lie is a lie; why be bothered by it?

And slowly, slowly, silently watching, Gurdjieff became more aware of his reactions rather than the actions of others.

Every situation is an opportunity to take time to be silent, to take some time for yourself. *Being silent helps you become aware of what you are doing, of what is happening to you. It creates distance.* If someone insults you, become aware. What is happening to you when the insult reaches you? Be silent and understand yourself — this changes everything. Normally when someone insults us, we concentrate on the person: "Why is he insulting me? How can I take revenge?" We forget ourselves completely; the other becomes the focus. This is missing an opportunity to focus on ourselves and bring in more awareness. When someone insults you, be silent and understand.

By giving ourselves this silent time, we create an opportunity for the truth to arise. If we are angry or in emotional turmoil, it is difficult to see the objective truth of the situation. If the mind is whirling with defenses, with reactions, we cannot see clearly. It is just as if you have thrown a rock into a still, clear pond. The water becomes muddied; turmoil is created. After a while, the mud settles to the bottom of the pond, the ripples smooth out, and all is calm and clear again. We need to allow time for things to settle. Then we can see clearly, and we move into choiceless awareness — of the total picture, of the truth — and therefore our course of action is obvious.

Love yourself. Once you are grounded in your own love, your own aloneness, the same quality persists, whether or not you are in a relationship. Love becomes your state of being. All your relationships are greatly enhanced, including, most important, your relationship with yourself!

⊕ FOUR-MINUTE MEDITATION: *How Do I Love?*

BENEFITS

This technique brings you to a deeper understanding of yourself and your ability to give and receive love.

Focus on the question: "How *do* I love?" or "How would I like to be able to love?" Here we deal with a crucial aspect of our life and being. It is in the ability or inability to love that more of us feel either strong or crippled than probably in any other area. How do I love? Do I wish I could love more? What makes me wish this? What holds me back? What do I fear in loving? How valid are these fears?

Work with this for four minutes a day for a week. Then, if you find it valuable, keep doing it. When you come upon understandings about yourself with compassionate nonjudgment, allow time to absorb them and rest quietly within yourself.

MEDITATION: *Sixty-Second Stop*

BENEFITS

> *This powerful yet simple technique encourages the love in your heart to grow, and it attracts more love to you.*

Close your eyes and become aware of your heart. It might help to place your hand on your heart. Bring in a memory of a person, place, or event that brings you joy. Feel the happiness filling your heart with that memory.

Do this technique whenever you are feeling disconnected from your heart or whenever you want to increase the love in your heart.

FOUR-MINUTE MEDITATION: *Two Kinds of Love* ✵

BENEFITS

> *As our dependency for "need-love" lessens, we become more deeply rooted in ourselves. We learn the difference between loneliness and aloneness. Loneliness is absence of the other. Aloneness is the presence of oneself.*

There are two kinds of love: need-love and gift-love. Need-love depends on another person; it is immature love. Gift-love depends on us; it is mature love. With the first the emphasis is on how to get more. With the second the emphasis is on how to give more. We become mature the moment we start giving rather than needing.

Focus on understanding yourself, allowing both need-love and gift-love to be present. Over time, as we mature, need-love transforms into gift-love. Then love is not a relationship; it is a state of being.

⊙ FOUR-MINUTE MEDITATION: *Emphasis on the Heart*

BENEFITS

This technique will take you deep into your heart, where wisdom, peace, and contentment reside.

Focus on your heart. It is through feeling, not through thinking, that we arrive at love. It is through emotions that we feel the divine for the first time, not through argumentation. The heart quenches thirst, it gives contentment. Put logic aside and follow love. Whenever there is a choice between logic and love, choose love. Bring love in. Choose a specific situation in which you have a decision to make or in which you are in a fight with yourself or someone else. Focus on your heart. Breathe . . . feel . . . breathe . . . feel . . . and wait patiently. The solution arises from the wisdom of your heart. If it does not come the first time, do this technique for several days until the answer arises.

DRUNK WITH THE DIVINE:
THE SILENCE OF THE SOUL

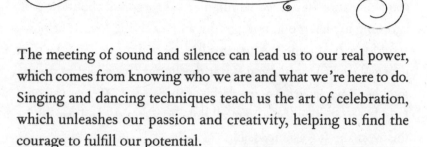

The meeting of sound and silence can lead us to our real power, which comes from knowing who we are and what we're here to do. Singing and dancing techniques teach us the art of celebration, which unleashes our passion and creativity, helping us find the courage to fulfill our potential.

Simultaneously and paradoxically, music takes us to the silence of our soul. Here we have the complementariness of opposites: sound and silence. We need both to nourish us and to give us a form of expression. Sages through the ages have loved music and dancing. Whatever the religion or cult, in whatever part of the world, music seems to be the center of ceremony or ritual — and often singing or chanting or intoning along with it. For the Sufis, music is a source of their meditation. They experience an unfolding of the soul, an opening of the intuitive faculties. Their hearts open to all the beauty that is within and without, uplifting them and at the same time bringing them that contentment for which every soul yearns.

I Love You

"And I loooooooove you" I sang enthusiastically as I wove my way through the circle of oncoming dancers. Participating in a Sufi dancing workshop, which involved learning simple mantras and then singing them in a circle or to a simple dance formula, I was thoroughly enjoying myself. Suddenly I found myself face-to-face with the girlfriend of my recent ex-boyfriend, "the other woman." This was the woman he had left me for! Since I had not yet fully recovered, I was at first taken aback to see her. Then I found my-self looking into her face and singing "I love you," which were the words of the song we were singing. In those seconds a profound transformation happened within me — I forgot all about the pain and sung my heart out, both giving and receiving love. The pow-erful force of singing the mantras had carried me beyond the pain into a place of love and joy. After the singing we all sat in silence together. I was amazed at the depth of the silence. We were all one; I could *feel* it. And if we were all one, how could I feel hatred for this woman? It was impossible.

When you sing and chant (and dance), your heart opens; you naturally feel trust and are ready to sit silently. Everything feels alright. When you become ecstatically alright you can sing your way to silence, peace, and calm. *When you sing together you breathe together.* Singing leads the way to the silence of your soul, the well-spring of your creativity. Singing vibrates every cell in your body, bringing you back into the body. It is a powerful, healing tool we can all use, whether or not we are "singers." We all have the ca-pacity to sing; we just need to bring more awareness to its power.

Music and Silence

Miten and Deva Premal, internationally renowned musicians and recording artists, have been friends of mine for more than twenty years. They give concerts worldwide to illustrate how music, chanting, humming, and singing can bring you to your inner si-lence. Their music is based on meditation, and they are longtime practitioners of the expressive techniques in this book. At their concerts they ask people not to clap, so at the end of the songs everyone can sit and enjoy the silence. No clapping means no separation — musician and audience are one. *The music is there to deepen the silence*; it is not there as entertainment (although it's fine if it does entertain you). It is not based on excitement. When music is based on meditation it comes from a deep place, a place of trust of whatever is right. There is no stress because it is not a performance. The music is born out of silence and goes back into silence. The true purpose of music based on meditation is to awaken a longing in the heart for that which is omnipresent: the experience of silence and meditation.

Miten and Deva Premal's music is also based on their experience of joy and celebration. As Miten puts it, "There are two reasons to play music. One is for ecstatic celebration. The other is to access deep inner silence. These are the peaks and the valleys, the two wings of the bird, roots and wings. Anything else is entertainment. If you use music as a sacred tool, it gives you ecstasy. You become the ecstasy and the silence, and it becomes you. The deeper you go into the ecstasy, the deeper you can go into silence."

I highly recommend buying Miten and Deva Premal's CDs and, even better, attending their concerts. (For more information, see p. 207.)

FOUR-MINUTE MEDITATION: *Music as Meditation* ✦

BENEFITS

Music is one of the easiest ways to discover meditation. Life is sound, and music can be used as a tool to connect us with deeper parts of ourselves. This enhances our creativity and joy. See my music recommendations on p. 207.

Choose some music that you particularly like, music that helps you relax. Close your eyes and listen to it. Allow the music to help you drop deeper inside. Music is a doorway to meditation. All you have to do is allow it to take you deeper. Notice how particular music vibrates well with your heart and soul.

Create more and more possibility around you for celebration; don't force the inner to be silent. By creating more and more festivity, singing, dancing around you, your inner silence naturally and automatically flowers within

FOUR-MINUTE MEDITATION:
Feel Yourself in the Center of Sound

BENEFITS

Over time, you hear the silence even amid the roar of a city. You become calmer and more relaxed, more in tune with the present moment, more joyful for no reason.

Sit and listen to all the sounds around you. Feel yourself at the center of them all. Use the sounds to bring you back to the moment. As you pay attention to the sounds, you start to notice the silence in between them. *Often we hear, but we don't listen.* Close your eyes and bring awareness to the sounds and then to the silence in between the sounds. We are born into an ocean of silence and sound. Every sound is included in the silence, yet *no sound disturbs the silence.* Although the world will never be quiet for us, we can remain connected to the silence that is always there. If you can, go to a park, to the beach, to the hills, to a forest, or to the mountains. Any place in nature is an easy place to start.

I also recommend doing the Humming (p. 132) or the Dancing (p. 28) meditation.

THE BUSINESS OWNER'S TALE:
SILENCE AT WORK

Are you wired and tired?

My student Mark owns a recycling business. He has ten employees and four shareholders and owns four large trucks. When
he first started, he had only one or two people working for him. He
vacillated between being too nice and being overcontrolling, from
being too hard to being a pushover. As a result, he usually ended
up without a worker or with workers who acted out their frustrations on the job. Something was missing. Mark took a good look
at his life and saw that he was, as he says, "wired and tired." He
was chain-smoking and obsessed with "making it." He told me
that he could hardly find a moment to breathe and that even if he
did find the time, he wouldn't know how to relax. Something
didn't compute. Enter the power of silence.

Mark thought he had to choose between meditation and all the
other parts of his life, thinking that meditating wasn't something
businesspeople did. He decided to start with a four-minute meditation every morning before going to work. He particularly liked
Watch Rush Hour Go By (p. 125) and the One-Minute Gibberish
(p. 125). Mark learned to stop, if only for a short while at first, *iden-
tifying* with the mind's goals, beliefs, and intents. Slowly he slipped
into a space of *not knowing*, of not having the answers. He began
to rediscover that cool, silent place within, beyond the grip of any
inner or outer noise, where he could deeply relax and view his life

with perspective and clarity. Mark saw that running a business was just part of the journey, nothing more, nothing less. Your business is not you, but it can be your unfoldment and your teacher. People who are working for you start working *with* you, because you *let* them! You allow the space for trust. People need direction, but they don't want to be controlled. Right actions and mutual respect become its new foundations.

Mark also discovered the power of silence when communicating and negotiating. Sometimes it is more creative to say nothing, or to say less. By learning to allow silence, Mark earned the trust and the respect of his employees. The business ran more smoothly and transformed itself from an organization based on fear and control to a productive, dynamic organism.

Especially in the business world, we are trained to think that being powerful means being able to respond quickly. We think we have to know what to do at every moment. But practicing silence shows us that true power often comes from taking the extra moments to hear what's in our hearts and minds and to listen to our deepest wisdom.

MEDITATION: *Emails*

BENEFITS

This technique saves you time and, depending on the circumstances, money. Communication and relationships are enhanced, and you have an easy way to include meditation in your busy day. You can use this practice with other written communications and for reading emails as well as writing them.

Do you sometimes find that you move too quickly and forget details? As one example, these days so many of us are inundated with emails, and they can be a real source of tension.

The next time you write an email, stop for a moment and take a deep breath before you start. Allow yourself to relax by dropping your shoulders down, feeling your feet on the ground, and settling comfortably into your chair. Now write your email, staying fully present with what you are writing and with the person you are writing to. Write in a relaxed way with full awareness. If you are in a hurry, include the awareness that you are in a hurry.

When finished, reread the email, checking the content, spelling, and attachments, if there are any. Breathe and pause for a moment before you hit Send.

LONGER SILENCE MEDITATIONS

This final section includes some "recipes" for finding quiet time for reflection, for contemplation, for being silent with ourselves or in a small group. Each of these can be done alone, though I recommend trying a small group of friends as well. Group meditations give us the opportunity to experience what it's like to be alone yet not alone, and to explore the difference between loneliness and aloneness. This brings healing and understanding and helps us discover the anchor of love and wisdom that resides within us all.

MEDITATION: *An Evening of Silence*

Evening is the time of day when, for many of us, work is over. It's a wonderful time to reflect — to absorb, to assimilate our experiences, to release the tensions of the day and relax into ourselves. And because we're already used to "downshifting" in the evening, devoting an evening to silence is an easy way to bring balance to our lives. A periodic evening of silence will keep you sane. It also helps to prevent insomnia.

Of course, there are any number of ways to structure your evening — or not structure it. But here are some of my favorite ideas for spending an evening in silence. You can do these alone or with a few friends. The same principles apply.

First, in preparation, arrange to take the kids to a friend's house, and give your spouse or housemates advance notice about what you'll be doing for the evening.

Have your favorite food and beverages on hand.

When you arrive home, take a shower. Wash off the day, and refresh body and spirit. Or perhaps take a bath or sit in a hot tub, if you have one. Water helps us to relax and releases tensions from the body and mind. Put on fresh, comfortable clothes. Turn off the phone, leave the mail. This is a no-reading, no-emails, no-Internet night. *Relaxation means no more information going in.*

Spend a few minutes before dinner doing your favorite "non-doing" thing. Sit on the porch with a cup of tea or a cool fruit juice. Turn down the lights in your favorite room and listen to some soothing, wordless music. Take your time; there's no hurry.

If you spent the day sitting at a desk, before eating you might like to try an expressive meditation technique, for example the Shaking (p. 128) or the Dancing (p. 28). These are great as end-of-the-day methods to release mental, emotional, or physical stress. Or you might like to try some simple techniques such as Silence of the Night (p. 175) or Sit Silently and Wait (p. 174), or one of my guided meditation CDs: *Wisdom of the Body* or *Opening to Love* (see p. 206).

Prepare dinner slowly and meditatively, enjoying the process. Enjoy your food. You are not on a schedule. Be totally present with what you are eating. Don't do anything else; only eat your food.

Discover how silence helps you hear your body's messages.

Then allow the evening to unfold spontaneously. Remember, you are experimenting with how to belong to yourself, how to re-discover your inner silence. It doesn't matter what activity, or non-activity, you choose. *What matters is the quality of your presence with yourself.* Try not to have a "plan." You might sit on a chair all evening doing nothing, or you might do a variety of different activities. Your life is probably already overloaded with schedules. Tonight just let your *being* decide what you do, rather than the *mind.* Let each moment evolve out of the preceding moment.

This is an opportunity to discover what *you* feel and think rather than being constantly bombarded with other people's requests, comments, projections. This creates a space to digest the day and let things be and yourself be.

Savor each moment. Enjoy everything about it. You have given yourself this evening. Enjoy the sounds and sights and the feeling of freedom — you can do what you like. Do only what brings you joy — and do it only if you feel like doing it. (Think about how easily and spontaneously children move from one activity to the next.) Be careful not to fall into doing something "useful" out of a desire not to "waste time." Only do things your instinct guides you to do. You might take a walk, jog, garden, do nothing, or paint, draw, dance. When we take each moment as it comes, we encourage our creativity. You might be surprised as your inner poet, painter, or dancer arises to play. Be kind and gentle with yourself.

Above all, *enjoy* your evening. This is not about torture, not about forcing or trying. Nor is it a serious, gloomy, or austere affair. It's about relaxation and becoming more awake to ourselves with compassion and nonjudgment.

Don't set yourself impossible goals. In fact, don't set any goals. Just let happen what happens. And whatever happens will be perfect. There's nothing you *should* be doing; there's simply what you *are* doing at any given moment.

TWENTY-FOUR HOURS: *Silence at Home*

As the title suggests, this technique involves a full day and night of silence. I like to do this one with a few friends approximately every two or three months. While I always enjoy spending an evening in silence, there's something about spending a full day in silence that allows you to drop much deeper down. You gain deeper insight into and understanding of the gates of heaven and the gates of hell (for both will arise), and you gain clarity and perspective on the things that may be troubling you.

I always find that when I begin the day with a large bag of problems, by the end of the day either they've disappeared or creative solutions have arisen. As the swirling, muddy waters of emotional turmoil and mental unrest settle throughout the day into a calm, clear lake of silence, I notice that a transformation has taken place within me. My mind is clear, my heart is relaxed, and I am once again at home with myself, enjoying being me.

Doing this practice at home has the added benefit of bringing the extraordinary blessings of silence into the setting of my ordinary life, which helps remind me, especially when life gets hectic, that I always have silence within me to keep me calm and that I can always *choose* silence even when I'm chopping vegetables or sitting in my backyard. There is also something about being silent in a place where one spends a lot of time that emphasizes the fact that our deepest wisdom is always available. It's dependent not on a place but on our becoming more aware of its presence and how we can access it daily. The more we incorporate silence into our ordinary lives, the more it will sustain us when things get chaotic, and the more meaning and creativity will arise into each moment, whether we're doing dishes at the kitchen sink, cleaning the bathroom mirror, or tidying the living room.

It's tempting to believe that silence belongs only to the enlightened few or that you need to go traipsing off to more "meditative" places, but a full day in silence allows us to understand that our destination is never a place but rather a new way of looking at things.

Many people ask, "Is it really possible to spend twenty-four hours in silence at home? Won't I get distracted and start cleaning out the closets?" Just do it. You may be surprised at how good it feels to devote this kind of time to yourself.

You can do this practice alone, but I would recommend doing it with a group, preferably a few friends. Most people find it easier to go deeper inside knowing they are with others doing the same. It feels safer.

Being silent together can help friends rediscover each other. After all, sometimes all our verbiage gets in the way, and being silent allows us to communicate in more direct and attentive ways. Without the fast pace of language we can drop down to a deeper level, from the mind to the heart. In fact, remaining silent while in a group reveals to us how much we communicate nonverbally. You may be amazed at how well you communicate without words. Suddenly you are aware of how powerful a loving look can be, a hand on your shoulder, a wink, a smile; you see how funny a wordless gesture can be. We become more receptive to the messages people are sending us — a warm smile, kindness in someone's eyes. Instead of yakking away with idle conversation, *we have the opportunity to be with one another and not fill the silence but feel it.*

Choosing to be alone in silence for twenty-four hours, on the other hand, encourages us to get comfortable with solitude and deeper self-reflection. One of my clients, who works for a newspaper and is surrounded by noise and busyness all day, prefers to do this practice alone. Another client, who works mostly alone and wants to relate with people on a deeper level than the usual superficial "Hello, how are you?" prefers to do this with a group of friends.

Whether you're doing this alone or with a few friends, make sure to choose a setting where you won't be interrupted and where everyone present is a part of your experiment. If you live with others, you will want to forewarn them. Or they may want to join you. If you are driving to and from the location, drive in silence — no radio, CDs, or cell phones. Once there, turn off the phone, fax machine, computer. Put the mail aside for later. No listening to the radio, watching TV, or reading. You don't want any information coming into the mind.

If others are around, don't feel that you can't make eye contact or smile. All nonverbal communication is fine. But don't cheat by writing notes. If something essential comes up, for example, if you smell smoke and think the house might be burning down, by all means say so. But only say what is essential. This is a time to give to yourself. You deserve to receive your own love and kindness.

Initially, when people are still perhaps feeling a bit awkward, there will likely be some giggling and laughing. You might even find yourselves spontaneously falling into a laughing meditation. Let this happen. It's good. Laughing is always a release of tension. It breaks the ice and helps people feel comfortable with each other. Crying is okay too. Allow feelings to arise, accepting them with compassionate nonjudgment. If someone weeps or is sad, surround them with loving-kindness, but don't be invasive. If anger comes up, express it using one of the expressive meditations.

Be playful, enjoy yourselves, have fun. And remember: this is an experiment to discover more about yourself. Try not to be pulled outside yourself too much by the presence of others. Keep the focus on *you*.

Pay attention to your body, listening to its messages. You will discover many new things about yourself.

One technique I particularly like to do on a silent retreat is called the Reverberation of a Bell. It's quite simple. Find some chimes that make a really good sound. From time to time during the twenty-four hours, maybe at the beginning and end of a formal meditation technique, before and after lunch, and so on, sound the chimes. Notice how they reverberate through your body and soul. Bring awareness to how you *feel the sound in your belly*. Reverberating sounds are great for invoking our deeper wisdom.

Meals should be simple, light, and attractive. Choose foods

such as salads, soups, and fruits. Drink no caffeine, and try to use honey instead of sugar, which is a stimulant. If you're with a group, I suggest putting people on a roster to prepare meals and do the dishes. You could also arrange to have potluck meals to minimize cooking and dishes. People can, of course, eat together at a table or, if there is a garden, backyard, balcony, or veranda, they can take their food and eat by themselves.

Pay attention to how it feels to wash dishes, chop vegetables, and prepare food in this silent meditative context. See if it gives you a different take on "chores." They probably won't seem nearly as much like drudgework. In fact, you may even find that you enjoy just being present with yourself as you carry out these tasks. See if you can bring this awareness back into your daily life.

For those who prefer some structure, I've put together a loose schedule for your day. This schedule works well, whether you are alone or with others. If you are with a group, you might like to schedule some meditation techniques and let people know that they are free to do or not do them as they choose.

Don't feel bound by the schedule; it is meant only as a guide. Go wherever you are led. This is an experience to be enjoyed, to discover yourself, so have as few rules as possible.

If a full day indoors doesn't appeal to you, or you are doing this technique by yourself, you could spend the day out in nature: walking through the woods, napping, sitting, doing nothing. Watch the leaves falling to the ground, listen to the birds in the sky, absorb the silence of whatever part of nature is available to you. Or try some combination of formal meditations and unstructured time.

Sample Schedule for a Twenty-Four-Hour Silent Retreat

8:00–9:00 AM: At this time of day I suggest an expressive or more cathartic technique so the body can express itself and release physical, mental, or emotional tensions. You might try the Laughter (p. 9), Gibberish (p. 65), Osho Dynamic (p. 70), or Dancing (p. 28) meditation (CDs are available for all the meditations suggested here). It might seem like a contradiction to suggest techniques in which you make sounds, but the idea here is that this is a nontalking day. Sounds are okay. This is an opportunity to free yourself from the constant verbalizing of the mind and to drop to a deeper place inside. All the techniques I suggest here help you do that, because they bypass the conscious mind (which can be judgmental and controlling) and access the wisdom of your heart, body, and soul. The paradox is that when you *start* with the noise (the problem) it leads you to inner silence (the solution.)

9:30 AM: Breakfast

11:00 AM–12:00 PM: Sit silently for fifteen to forty-five minutes, followed by fifteen minutes of soft dancing (with eyes closed). If you are in a group, perhaps one of you can agree to sound a chime fifteen and then thirty minutes into the silent sitting to remind people to come back to the present moment. (Or use my *Witnessing the Mind* CD; see p. 206.)

12:30 PM: Lunch

2:30–3:30 PM: Try a quieter technique after lunch, such as the Humming meditation (p. 132), or try my *Wisdom of the Body* or *Opening to Love* CD (see p. 206).

4:30–5:30 PM: This is a good time for doing something expressive and celebratory. You might try the Laughter or the Dancing meditation (pp. 9, 28).

7:00 PM: Dinner

8:00 PM: Take your time to enjoy nightfall, to experience the restfulness of evening, and to assimilate your experiences of the day, either by taking a walk, journaling, or simply being. Or you might like to do the Silence of the Night (p. 175), Emphasis on the Heart (p. 156), or Looking without Judging (p. 141) meditation.

In the morning, you might like to have breakfast as a group and discuss your experiences. Or, if you have done the technique alone, you might want to do some journaling to record your experiences or share them with a friend.

As you go back to your normal routine, bring awareness to yourself. One of the gifts of silence is awareness. Notice the quality of your presence with friends, family, and colleagues after this day in silence. Many friends and clients tell me how relaxed and refreshed they feel afterward, as if they have been on vacation. One client told me how she walked straight into a tense situation between her two children and the babysitter. By listening with silent attentiveness to the problem, she quickly found a way to resolve it. She noticed how much better she handled the situation than she usually did — she had more patience, was more relaxed, and didn't react. Rather, she was able to create a space for everyone to express themselves, and a solution arose. This is creativity — the power of silence in relationship. Silence distills the art of listening and inspires creativity, dramatically improving the quality of our interactions.

Of course, all the suggestions listed above are just that: suggestions. Experiment and see what works for you. This is your twenty-four hours. If you enjoy this meditation, do it often. There's nothing quite like taking a full day out of our hectic lives and just being with ourselves in silence to help bring us into balance, to restore, rebuild, renew.

ADDITIONAL MEDITATIONS FOR SILENCE

BENEFITS

This technique can almost instantly bring you to awareness and help you relax. It helps you to remember yourself and to develop the qualities of the watcher. With regular practice, by and by a subtle relaxed alertness will begin to weave itself into your day.

It is so easy to lose ourselves in the activities of our day. If you stop your body totally, then the mind, because it has been taken unawares, also stops. And for those split seconds, with the mind stopped in its tracks, you are there, in the present moment.

You can do this meditation while walking along the street, folding laundry, or sorting files at the office. While you are engaged in one of these activities, stop. Freeze. For thirty seconds just be present with whatever is happening. Are you breathing? How does your body feel? Where is your mind? Where are you? In the present? The past? The future? Watch, observe, and notice yourself, without judgment. Then continue with your activity.

You can do this technique by yourself or with a friend. You might ask your friend to surprise you with a thirty-second stop when you're walking down the street together. Or you can do it yourself anytime — at work, on the bus, in the grocery store, in an elevator, doing the dishes. But remember, it must be done suddenly.

FOUR-MINUTE MEDITATION: *Sit Silently and Wait*

BENEFITS

As you practice doing nothing, by and by an understanding starts to arise between you and the meditative state. As this understanding grows you start to feel a subtle quality of relaxation, of serenity, woven into your whole day.

A meditative awareness comes like a whisper, not a shout. It comes with noiseless footsteps. If you are full of preoccupations, busyness, and noise, this awareness might appear, but it will leave again. Sit, close your eyes, and wait. Don't do anything; just sit in great waiting with an open, trusting heart. Then, if something is to "happen," you are ready to receive it. If nothing happens, at least you've had this downtime to do nothing. No matter what, after sitting silently for a while you feel more in touch with yourself, more peaceful.

It works best to do this at the same time every day. It doesn't matter what time you choose, but setting aside a time every day, say, in the early morning, as a midmorning break, or during your lunch hour, helps make it part of your daily routine. When the inner consciousness knows that the outer consciousness is waiting for it, there is a greater possibility of a meeting.

FOUR-MINUTE MEDITATION: *Stillness*

BENEFITS

In your utter helplessness, in your surrender, you find inner silence and stillness. This is the real silence that transforms, not the silence that you try to impose on yourself. And how can your doing go deeper than your being? All has stopped. The mind spins no more thoughts. And that silence is being. *You have arrived home.*

Striving after stillness creates confusion. Stillness cannot be achieved: it is already there. There is really nothing to be done. *Only being will transform you, not doing.*

Sit and just be. Or stand and just be. For a few moments allow the inner stillness to be there. *It is there already — just allow it.* If the mind is too busy, or if the emotions are in turmoil, then try one of the expressive meditations, for example, the Laughter (p. 9) or Gibberish (p. 65), and then be still. These techniques help you to release tensions and then just be, suffused with stillness.

FOUR-MINUTE MEDITATION: *Silence of the Night* ✪

BENEFITS

Night is so beautiful and a good time for meditation. It helps you release the tensions of the day easily, effortlessly.

Before you go to bed, alone or with a partner, sit silently, looking into the darkness. Become one with the dark; disappear into it. Look at the stars — feel the distance, the silence, the emptiness — and use night for your meditation. Sit on your bed, or on your balcony, or in your garden, doing nothing...just feeling, just being there. The day is worldly; the night is more spiritual. Over time you feel tremendously in tune with night. The world is asleep. Everything stops; all is quiet. People, with all their problems and complexities, have all disappeared into sleep. The atmosphere is clean, with no jarring note.

Start enjoying the beauty of the night. Absorb the tranquility, serenity, and comfort night offers. Your sleep then carries a quality of meditation, and in the morning you feel refreshed in a whole new way.

PART FOUR

Moving Forward

This is the beginning for you now, as you step out from the pages of this book and into the rest of your life. The new you is emerging from what you are absorbing and will continue to absorb from these pages. You can keep coming back to try different techniques and to reread sections that resonate with you — something I highly recommend. There is a lot to take in, and it's good to have fun and to take action steps one at a time. You are walking a different path now, a path of self-awareness, of self-love, of fun. Take the simplicity and wisdom of this book into your everyday life. Have you noticed a difference in yourself between the time when you first started reading and right now? Already your self-love and self-awareness have increased. Take a moment *now* to take that in. When you do these kinds of practices *consistently*, you experience a profound difference.

I encourage you to immediately start discovering yourself and to begin living the life of your dreams. I want you to succeed, to love your life. The practice of meditation is an integral part of success. A calm mind and open heart help you get the results you've been looking for. The areas of your life that will benefit are your health; your finances; all your relationships, including those with colleagues, family, and friends; your career; your creativity; and your spirituality.

THE NEW YOU!

The only certain thing in life is change. When people or situations change, you can fight the change and struggle upstream, or you can accept it. The spiritual purpose of change is to call us to develop qualities we didn't know we had. Change is a gift to our soul, allowing it to unfold and mature, allowing it to enrich us. If we push against something we create more resistance and more pain. Everything happens to teach us so that we can grow into who we truly are. Bless what you have. Everyone has a diamond mine of resourceful qualities and creativity within them. Sometimes the diamonds pop up easily; sometimes we have to dig deep to find them. If in a difficult situation, you can ask yourself what quality you need to find within yourself to create a positive outcome.

Every crisis is a crossroads. It is an end of one world and the beginning of another.

Every ending is followed by a beginning. You are on the threshold of something much bigger, which existence knows you are ready for. The new is always a million times better than the old. All spiritual growth is experienced by letting go of false concepts, beliefs, and programs in the mind so that we can stand in who we truly are. Everything we need we already have. Find the courage to lead *your* life — not the life other people want you to have, but the life you want to have. After all, it's your life, isn't it?

Put Yourself at the Top of Your To-Do List!

If you don't, you will start to feel resentful as your well runs dry. Fill your own well first. Only then can you give to others, and they will receive only the overflow, not your reserve tank. When I first started to meditate, I began with two minutes a day. With a busy family life it was all I thought I could do, and it proved to be a very powerful way to put myself at the top of my to-do list. Over time I found I could make more time for myself, and my family benefited as a result. I started to sing my own song, the song of the authentic me. Suddenly life was fun again, and everything flowed with more grace and ease. Guilt disappeared as I practiced not judging myself. I was showing up in my own life. After all, 80 percent of success is showing up.

One good way to help yourself be more present to yourself is to write down all your achievements. Start when you were very young and think of all your achievements since then. Don't just pick the big things; write down all the things you take for granted. You can also create a log of everyday successes and review it when you are faced with a new challenge. By writing it all down every day, you're reminding yourself of how worthy and valuable you are.

FOUR-MINUTE MEDITATION: *Be Open to Experiencing* ✦

BENEFITS

The beauty of experience is that the experience is always open, because further exploration is possible. Your experience is growing, changing, moving. It is continuously moving from the known into the unknown and from the unknown into the unknowable. Experience contains a beauty that can take you deep into meditation.

Meditation is just the beginning of a totally different world where joy, playfulness, compassion, nonjudgment, and sincerity have entered.

First you need to bring an *openness to experience*. Often people have prejudices about something, for example, about dancing as meditation. The first quality of a meditator is this openness to experience. Never believe anything unless you have experienced it for yourself.

Do dancing as meditation (p. 28). Put any prejudices aside, any questions such as, "How can meditation come out of dancing," and experiment with this technique.

Or experiment with something you think you can't do or that you feel you have a prejudice about.

TAKE ACTION

Great ideas depend on action, don't they? If you take no action, the idea remains in your head. What a waste! Beautiful ideas, such as inner peace, wealth, love, and happiness, are great. But it is not enough to dream; you must also act. You have to become involved; you have to be committed.

If you are convinced of some truth, act on it immediately! The mind is cunning, and the greatest cunningness of the mind is postponement. It says *tomorrow*. It says, "Yes, someday we are going to meditate. Let us first understand what meditation is." You can go on understanding what meditation is your whole life and never act. And unless you act, nothing is ever going to happen. Unless you start *doing* some of the techniques in this book, you will not experience the rewards they offer.

It feels safer to listen or watch others. Meditation becomes a kind of entertainment — spiritual entertainment! — but is utterly useless to you unless you participate. When you are around an inspirational person, or reading an inspirational book, it is not a question of taking the words seriously. It is a question of seeing the authenticity of the words and then acting on them. If an idea stirs your heart, if a bell starts ringing in your heart, then follow it. Go deeper into it, because that is the only way to be transformed. That is the only way to come home to yourself.

What Stops Us from Taking Action?

Fear has a paralyzing effect and can keep us frozen in doubt and despair. If you can let go of the story you are telling yourself about why the fear is there, and just see fear as an energy that has gotten stuck, then you can free yourself. What help most with fear are love and laughter. The Laughter meditation (p. 9) is a powerful way to break the grip of fear and take you into greater courage and passion for life.

It is deep trust that takes you into action. Action is risky. To talk about doing something is simple, but to move into action is risky because no map exists. In fact, nobody can be certain about the results of their actions. Think about Christopher Columbus. In those days people thought the world was flat and that you would fall off if you came to the edge. Columbus took action, sailed into his fear, and discovered a whole new world. The same can happen for you. Take action, walk into your fears, and act in spite of them. You discover a whole new world. If you don't act, how will you ever know if your idea could have come to fruition? *Only action proves that you trust, and only action can transform you.* Your choice is either to spend the rest of your life wondering if it would have worked or to do it. If it fails, good. At least you tried. You can now totally drop it, which frees you up to move on to the next thing. Unless you have a tremendous trust in life, unless you trust your inner voice, you can't go on the journey of the uncharted sea.

Take One Action a Day

Every day take at least one action step toward your dreams. Dreams don't usually happen overnight. When you consistently take action steps toward your goals they happen. If you feel lethargic, fatigued, run around the block seven times, or as many times as you can. It will help to get your energy moving. Come back and take your one action step for the day.

FOUR-MINUTE MEDITATION: *Befriend Failure*   ⬡

BENEFITS

This technique helps you gain confidence in yourself. Life wants you to succeed, to be happy. We mature through failure, we become more compassionate, and our sense of humor and our creativity are enhanced.

If you do not succeed, then get up and try again. Do not see failure as the end. Failure is just a stepping-stone, and much can be learned from it. Change your attitude. See failure as a good thing.

Recall a situation when you feel you failed, when things didn't go your way. Sit with yourself and look deeply into it. Be grateful you had this opportunity. See what you can learn from it. Acknowledge yourself for trying.

Running, Jogging, and Working-Out Meditations

The following techniques build on physical workout routines and can help tremendously when your energy feels stuck. Transforming your workout into a meditation simply takes a shift in awareness. Many people still hang on to the idea that meditation has to be done quietly and in stillness, that activity and meditation can't mix. I'd like to put those ideas to rest once and for all. *Any* activity can become a meditation if it is done with awareness.

Actually, movement *facilitates* awareness. Think about it: it's much easier to stay alert when you're moving than when you're sitting or lying down. The big challenge is to keep from going on automatic pilot, to keep from becoming mechanical. You may be a phenomenal runner, but if it's all technique, you've missed the point.

If you're a runner, run with awareness; if you work out at a gym, work out with awareness; if you're a jogger, jog with awareness. If you feel that your workout has become too routine, do something different. Whenever we are learning something new, or are not yet expert at it, we have to pay more attention, we have to be more aware. Experiment with a movement that creates awareness in you, perhaps dancing. *The point to remember is that movement creates awareness.* Once it stops creating awareness, then it is of no use to you anymore. Change to another activity where you will have to be alert again.

MEDITATION: *Running*

Humans have been running for thousands of years, because we were hunters, and when we start running the body/mind engages with that primal layer of consciousness. Running can be an especially powerful tool for meditators, since it creates a possibility to go very deep into ourselves.

If you are new to running, I recommend that you run in the mornings, when the air is fresh and the day is just coming alive. Of course, you will want to consider any health problems you might have and to speak with your doctor if you have any questions about whether or not you should run. It's also very important that you wear good running shoes.

Start with a half mile, then one mile, then build up to at least three miles. Run using your whole body, including your hands. Breathe deeply and from the belly.

When you are running fast, breathing deeply, inhaling and exhaling, after a while the division between mind and body starts to disappear. You become unified. When you are running and the breathing has taken hold of you, worries suddenly disappear. You simply cannot be fully engaged with running and worried at the same time.

MEDITATION: *Jogging*

Jogging is similar to running, except that for many it's more enjoyable. It may seem that jogging is simply running at a slower pace, but there's a different mind-set to jogging. It's a leisurely run done at a pace that's right for you. You appreciate your surroundings and the way you feel. Jogging is a pleasurable exercise that anyone can do and enjoy. Running takes you farther faster, although as I have explained above, both can be a thoroughly enjoyable physical workout *and* a meditation at the same time. It's purely a matter of personal preference.

Jogging follows the same principle as running. You want to breathe deeply and stay aware that "right now I am jogging." Again, I'd recommend jogging in the early morning. (Jogging can also be helpful at the end of the day to rid yourself of the day's tensions.) Enjoy the freshness of the day, filling your lungs as you breathe deeply. If your mind starts wandering, come back to the breathing and inhabit your body. As your body builds up a sweat, feel yourself becoming one with your body, and feel your mind disappearing. This is the body's opportunity to take over, at least temporarily, from the mind.

MEDITATION: *Working Out*

If you prefer going to the gym, I recommend that you develop a routine. Without a routine, it's too easy to drift — five minutes on this machine, five minutes on that machine — without ever dropping down deep. Having a routine also makes it harder to come up with excuses (you're too busy, you'd rather be having coffee, you've got another appointment). The specifics of your routine don't matter as much as simply *having* one.

Working out is an opportunity to be with yourself. Close your eyes, become aware of your breathing, inhabit your body, come into the present time. Perhaps short, shallow breaths will be needed at the beginning, then deeper breaths.

Be alert to yourself. Your breathing brings you down from the head and into the body. If you become aware of any emotions, for example, anger or sadness, let the body express and release them. Give your mind a break, and let the body take over.

Notice if you go on automatic, the body running on the treadmill and the mind back in the office. Gently remind yourself to come back into the body, focusing on the breathing, if this helps. Remember to practice nonjudgment of and compassion toward yourself. Slowly, slowly you can transform your exercising into meditation.

Use movement and exercise as a means to get in touch with deeper parts of yourself, and you will enter more easily and fully into the present moment.

GETTING STARTED: THREE-, SEVEN-, AND TWENTY-ONE-DAY PLANS

For those of you who are not sure how to get started, here are some ideas to work with. Adapt them to your lifestyle. To get the best results, set some time aside *every day*, and stick with a given practice for *three*, *seven*, or *twenty-one days*.

Choose one four-minute technique, and do it for three days, then see if you can continue for seven days, and then see if you can complete twenty-one days. At the beginning or end of the day is a good time, but, depending on your schedule, you might prefer lunchtime.

Give meditation a chance. The point of doing the same technique for at least three, and ideally twenty-one, days is to give it a chance. This strategy is much more effective than constantly switching back and forth, because it takes a while for the benefits to manifest. When you repeatedly do the same technique for at least three, seven, or twenty-one days you become so familiar with the technique that the focus can be on you instead of the technique. In fact, the technique serves as a doorway through which you enter and discover yourself. You get quicker results because the technique is always the same, but you are not. After twenty-one days, you may choose to stay with the same technique, or you may want to select a different one. Remember that you are discovering methods that you enjoy, that suit your lifestyle, and that work for you. We are all different. What works for your friend or spouse, for example, might not work for you. Never compare. Stay with your-self, and build your own unique practice.

Don't force it. Meditation should not be a forced effort, or it will be doomed from the start. Forcing creates a subtle tension, a contraction in the body.

Some of us are body oriented, some heart oriented, and some intellect oriented. The methods in this book can be used by all three types of people. Just choose a method that you enjoy, and go into it as deeply as possible. If you enjoy a method, it means it fits with you, that there is a subtle harmony between you and the tech-nique. You are much more likely to stick with your meditation practice if you find a practice that *you like.*

Experiment with different techniques. Once you have decided to bring more awareness into your life, start experimenting with the different techniques. Meditation techniques are a set of keys — not a series of answers. Try one and see if it fits (remembering to give it at least three and ideally twenty-one days). Let joy be the criterion for whether or not it is working for you. We have to begin somewhere. It may be a false beginning, but if we grope around enough, we'll find the door. So begin somewhere — it doesn't matter where. If you wait for the right beginning, then you will never begin at all. Just start!

Dealing with Stress: The Short Plan

Are you looking to meditation to help with stress? Meditation is good for your physical health, particularly for your heart. These techniques are some of the best "de-stressors" I know. Try the Short Plan any time you have a few minutes to spare. If your stress is particularly acute and/or you can find the time for the Longer Plan, do it. It gives deeper and more lasting results.

Laughter (p. 9)

or

Creating a Haven (p. 124)
or
Jogging (p. 184)

Dealing with Stress: The Longer Plan

Working Out (p. 185)
or
Osho Dynamic (p. 70)
or
Shaking (p. 128)

The Morning Plan

This might suit those of you who do shift work or who are willing
to get up earlier. In the mornings we are fresh and receptive to the
meditative state. Beginning with a meditation transforms the quality of your whole day.

Watch Rush Hour Go By (p. 125)
One-Minute Gibberish (p. 125)

The Love/Intimacy/Compassion Plan

If you are having problems with your relationship, or you just want
more love and intimacy in your life, try these techniques. They
are simple yet powerful resources to bring you more of what you
want. Love begins with loving yourself, so give yourself a treat
and bring more love into your life.

Emphasis on the Heart (p. 156)
Two Kinds of Love (p. 155)
Cherish Yourself, Cherish Others (p. 113)

The Dealing with Emotions Plan

One of the most effective ways to release pent-up emotions, including anger and frustration, is the Gibberish meditation. Wherever

you can find a suitable place, let it all out. One of my clients used to do this in her car at lunchtime. You will be amazed at how relaxed and calm you feel afterward. When the "charge" has been released, you can then approach situations with greater clarity of mind.

Gibberish (p. 65): two minutes of gibberish, two minutes of silent sitting

You might like to use my *Gibberish* CD (see p. 206).

The Finding Yourself Plan

Think of an issue that touches a nerve for you that you would like to bring more awareness to for one week. It might be a problem at work or with family or friends. Meditation can help bring clarity, so that creative solutions can arise. After one week, you might want to continue for one more week, or for one month until you feel complete with the exercise.

Sit Silently and Wait (p. 174)

The Travel Plan

When we travel we leave our normal routines — of diet, exercise, etc. — behind. Here are some suggestions to help with the stress of travel. You can do these anywhere, at any time, day or night.

Sometimes, when I'm in a crowded, chaotic airport waiting for a delayed flight (don't you just feel that frustration rising?), I listen to music with headphones, close my eyes, feel my feet on the ground, and breathe. When a situation is not in our control, instead of tensing up in anger, we can respond to it in a creative way for ourselves.

Breathe (p. 136)

Listen to Music (p. 145) (Use headphones. Music recommendations are on p. 207.)

Guided Relaxation and Meditation CD with music (p. 206)

Preparing for an Interview

Some of my clients have asked me for help getting ready for a job interview. I particularly recommend this meditation to help you feel calm, grounded, and self-confident. You might even remember during the interview to keep your legs uncrossed, to feel your feet on the ground, and to breathe. The more relaxed the body is, the more relaxed you are.

Sixty-Second Stop (p. 155)

Before a Meeting

Doing a short meditation technique before and at the end of a meeting can have a powerful effect on enhancing composure in a negotiation, on facilitating better communication and teamwork, and on encouraging new ways of seeing and doing projects.

One-Minute Creating a Haven (p. 124)

Whichever techniques you choose, relax and enjoy them. Meditation is not some serious or forbidding task; it is something to be enjoyed. The point is not to achieve anything but simply to discover yourself. Try to stay fully present. Any time you are fully present, you are meditating.

Remember too that meditation and relaxation build on themselves. It's only difficult in the beginning. Once you start paying attention to the meditative core of energy that is already within you, it grows. Eventually you reach that point of "effortless effort" as they describe it in the Zen tradition, where you are making an effort but everything flows so easily that your effort feels effortless.

OPEN YOUR HEART AND SHARE

Thank you for making meditation, laughter, and celebration priorities in your life. I hope that you now have a greater awareness of how to transform uncomfortable emotions into the joy, love, silence, and wisdom that reside within you.

My greatest joy comes from sharing the benefits I have gained from the techniques in this book. I have shared my story and those of others to inspire and encourage you to keep going, no matter what. You will be showered with blessings that you cannot even imagine right now. For ongoing support I invite you to join our Discover Meditation community at www.pragito.com. Sign up for the free weekly meditations and receive information about free teleseminars and other events and programs that keep you connected with us.

I want us to create an epidemic of laughter that reaches to the farthest corners of the earth. Imagine people everywhere laughing, crying, and being silent together. Imagine the love and compassion that will blossom. This is my vision for humanity that I invite you to become a part of. I hope you share my enthusiasm and begin to talk about the meditation techniques in this book with everyone you know. The more you share, the more your love, laughter, and celebration grow and the more your dreams come true. The birds and the trees, the flowers and the rivers, the mountains and the forests are already celebrating. Let's join them and together transform this beautiful earth into a paradise, one person at a time, beginning with you.

Acknowledgments

My special thanks to:

Osho, in gratitude.

Miten and Deva Premal, for your constant support of my work.

Joyce Arnowitz, for your love and your faith in the success of this book.

Elizabeth Evans, my literary agent, for your diligence and support.

Georgia Hughes, my editor at New World Library, for your skilled and insightful editing.

Osho International, for allowing me to enrich the text with a selection of Osho's meditation techniques from the book *Meditation: The First and Last Freedom.*

David Wood, for pushing me to come up with my best ideas.

Caroline Pincus, for your advice, warmth, and skilled editing.

Amy Rost, for your wonderful editing and insight.

John Gray, for your inspiration, encouragement, and support.

Karen West, for your enthusiasm and faith in my writing.

John Evarts, for your love and friendship.

Sasha the cat, for sitting in my office with me every day, bringing comfort and joy.

My son, Paul, for the life lessons we have shared. I love you.

And finally, to all the people whose lives were changed in such outrageous ways by the expressive meditation techniques that they became stories in this book.

Notes

Notes correspond to the page numbers listed in the left column.

Part I: Laughter

2 *"Laughter is a good natural tranquilizer..."* Raymond A. Moody Jr., MD, *Laugh after Laugh: The Healing Power of Humor* (Jacksonville, FL: Headwaters Press, 1978), 42.

17 *We master basic skills* so *that players can be intuitive...* Phil Jackson, *Sacred Hoops* (New York: Hyperion Press, 2006), 97.

Part II: Tears

50 *"The reason people feel better after crying..."* William H. Frey, MD, *Crying: The Mystery of Tears* (Minneapolis: Winston Press, 1985), 11.

93 *"hyper-anxious animal[s]..."* Ernest Becker, *The Denial of Death* (New York: Simon and Schuster, 1975), 115.

Part III: Silence

133 *Chants are actually metabolized into natural painkillers...* David Simon, MD, *Free to Love, Free to Heal: Heal Your Body by Healing Your Emotions* (San Diego: Chopra Enterprises, 2009), 83.

159 *"There are two reasons to play music..."* Interview with Miten, July 2006, Corte Madera, California.

Index

About the Author

Using the principles she teaches, Pragito Dove transformed her fear and grief into joy and inner peace. Dove is president of Discover Meditation Training Inc., a cutting-edge meditation training company. She trained extensively as a meditation master and spiritual teacher at the Osho Multiversity, Pune, India. She holds a master's degree in education from London University and certification as a Master Hypnotherapist and a Professional Hypnotherapy Instructor. Her first book, *Lunchtime Enlightenment* (Penguin Group, 2001), was published in five languages. An experienced trainer and facilitator, she has provided meditation training to organizations including the University of California San Francisco Cancer Resource Center, Hill Physicians Medical Group, the *San Francisco Chronicle*, NASA, Peak Potentials Training Inc., the John C. Lincoln Hospital, United Health Care, World Laughter Tour Inc., the Association of Applied Therapeutic Humor, Autodesk, and the National Association of Women Business Owners. She lives in Marin County, California. Visit her website at www.pragito.com.

Pragito.com

Visit the online world of Pragito Dove and Discover Meditation Training, Inc., and become a part of our online community.

Free weekly meditations
Free teleseminars
Practitioner certification trainings
Laughter meditation teletrainings
Discover Meditation coaching
Individual hypnotherapy sessions

Shop Online at the Pragito.com Store

At the Pragito.com store you can purchase a variety of books, audio and video programs, CDs, and DVDs.

Bestselling CDs include:
Guided Relaxation and Meditation
Opening to Love
Wisdom of the Body
Laughter and Tears
Gibberish
Insomnia
Witnessing the Mind

For additional information please write to or call:

Pragito Dove Trainings
PO Box 2144
Mill Valley, CA 94942
Email: info@pragito.com
Phone: (800) 919-3683

Recommended Audio CDs

The music or spoken-word CDs mentioned throughout the book
can be ordered from the following sources:

Deva Premal and Miten's music:
www.mitendevapremal.com

Shastro and Nadama's music:
www.malimba.com

Manish Viyas's music:
www.whiteswanmusic.com

Osho Meditation soundtracks:
www.pragito.com
www.osho.com

NEW WORLD LIBRARY is dedicated to publishing books and other media that inspire and challenge us to improve the quality of our lives and the world.

We are a socially and environmentally aware company, and we strive to embody the ideals presented in our publications. We recognize that we have an ethical responsibility to our customers, our staff members, and our planet.

We serve our customers by creating the finest publications possible on personal growth, creativity, spirituality, wellness, and other areas of emerging importance. We serve New World Library employees with generous benefits, significant profit sharing, and constant encouragement to pursue their most expansive dreams.

As a member of the Green Press Initiative, we print an increasing number of books with soy-based ink on 100 percent postconsumer-waste recycled paper. Also, we power our offices with solar energy and contribute to nonprofit organizations working to make the world a better place for us all.

Our products are available
in bookstores everywhere.
For our catalog, please contact:

New World Library
14 Pamaron Way
Novato, California 94949

Phone: 415-884-2100 or 800-972-6657
Catalog requests: Ext. 50
Orders: Ext. 52
Fax: 415-884-2199
Email: escort@newworldlibrary.com

To subscribe to our electronic newsletter, visit
www.newworldlibrary.com

HELPING TO PRESERVE OUR ENVIRONMENT

46,104
trees were saved

New World Library uses 100% postconsumer-waste recycled paper for our books whenever possible, even if it costs more. During 2008 this choice saved the following precious resources:

www.newworldlibrary.com

ENERGY	WASTEWATER	GREENHOUSE GASES	SOLID WASTE
32 MILLION BTU	17 MILLION GAL.	4 MILLION LB.	2 MILLION LB.

Environmental impact estimates were made using the Environmental Defense Fund Paper Calculator © www.papercalculator.org.